Oddbjørn By

MEMO

- The Easiest Way to Improve Your Memory

Lunchroom Publishing
Publisher of Intelligent Books

First Published in Australia in 2007

Copyright © Oddbjørn By 2007 - www.oby.no/au
Copyright © Lunchroom Publishing 2007

Illustrations © Siri J. Egeland 2007
Translation © Håkon By 2007
Cover design © Torfinn Solbrekke 2007
Set in Adobe Garamond by Lars Eirik Aase

Originally published in Norwegian under the title *Memo – den enkleste veien til bedre hukommelse*, copyright © 2006 Kagge Forlag AS, Oslo

All rights reserved. No part of this publication may be reproduced, stored in a retrieval system, or transmitted in any form or by any means, electronic, mechanical, photocopying, recording or otherwise, without the prior permission of the copyright owner.

Lunchroom Publishing Pty Ltd, PO Box 462, Double Bay NSW 1360, Australia
[p] (02) 8005 1462 [f] (02) 9475 0802
[e] lunchroom@iprimus.com.au [i] www.lunchroom.net.au

National Library of Australia
Cataloguing-in-Publication entry:

By, Oddbjørn, 1981- .
Memo: the easiest way to improve your memory.

Bibliography.
Includes index.
ISBN 9780980326901.

1. Mnemonics. 2. Learning strategies. 3. Instructional systems. I. Egeland, Siri J. II. Title.

153.14

Printed in Australia by Griffin Press

Contents

A memorable story... 9

How to read this book.. 17

How your memory works.. 21
    Journeys.. 24
    Remembering future events... 30

Here, there and everywhere... 37

Numerical Systems... 41
    The Single System... 41
    The Double System... 43
    The Alternative Double System (ADS)........................... 45
    The Triple System... 47
    Using Numerical Systems.. 51

Tips for memorising effectively... 57
    Listen carefully; I shall say this only once....................... 57
    Repetition... 57
    Concentration... 59
    Observation and attention.. 60
    Creating journeys.. 61

Memo for general knowledge and in school..................... 65
    Speed-reading.. 65
    History and dates.. 67
    Languages... 72

Geography.. 80
Anatomy.. 85
First Aid.. 87
Maths... 89
Biochemistry and organising knowledge......................... 92
Speed-studying: How to pass exams in two days................. 94
Oral exams... 101

Memo everyday.. 103
Remembering appointments....................................... 103
Weekly schedules.. 103
Agenda... 105
Birthdays, anniversaries and other important dates............ 106
Memorising manuscripts, speeches and texts.................... 108
Honey, where are the keys?....................................... 110
Remembering key points in conversations....................... 111
Jokes, riddles, quotes and stories................................ 112
Phone numbers... 114
Job interviews.. 116
Be better at sports by using your memory....................... 117
Parking.. 118
Directions... 120
Numbers and letters in general................................... 121
Music.. 123

Names and faces.. 127
Here and now... 127
Action... 129
Multiple names... 130

Memory tricks and competitions...................... 133
Memorising a deck of cards....................................... 134
Blackjack.. 137
How to always win make-a-match................................. 137
Which day of the week where you born?......................... 139

Pi (π) and long strings of numbers. 144

Other memory methods. **149**
The story method. 149
The link method. 150
Acronyms and mnemonic devices. 151
Poems. 152
The phonetic alphabet. 152
Networks. 153
Mapping your keywords. 155

Myths. **157**
Remembering vs understanding. 157
You only use ten percent of your brain. 158
Photographic memory exists. 159
We remember it all, we just need some help to retrieve it. . . . 162
Listen to Mozart while eating goat cheese. 163

Profiles and world records. **165**
Dominic O'Brien. 165
Andi Bell. 166
Simon Orton. 166
Ben Pridmore. 166
World records. 167

Appendix. **171**

If you are hooked. **179**
1 to 20 in Turkish. 179
Morse code. 181
Binary numbers. 183
Wonders of the World. 185
Countries and capitals inSouth America. 186

Bibliography. **187**
Acknowledgements. 188

A memorable story

Norway, Friday 28th of May 2004

An elderly man falls flat on his face on the cobblestones. Two girls run over to help him back on his feet. "Thank you," the man says, patting one of the girls on the shoulder.

The university can't afford to maintain the area around campus. I unlock my bike.

"Hi, Oddbjørn! Still going strong?"

"I'm great, Martin. I've just finished my history exam."

"Does that mean you're on holidays now?"

"No, I might do another exam. Extinct religions."

"But you don't study religion?"

"No, but two of my friends do. We're going to split the reading list and make keywords for each other."

"When's the exam?"

"Wednesday. Oral exam."

"So what do you know about extinct religions?"

"Jupiter…" A sparrow flies past, darting into a hole in the wall. "Venus …"

"I know you've taught yourself how to memorise decks of cards, numbers and the notes for your history exam, but no one can pass extinct religion in five days. Not without any prior knowledge. Have you ever shown your parents your high school results? The weather forecast's good for this weekend – you should come and play beach volleyball instead!"

Hours later, John chucks a fat tome into my lap.

"You do keywords on Roman religion, Oddbjørn. I'll read four hundred pages on the Greek and Sámi ones and Helena will do the same on Norse mythology, Mesopotamian and Egyptian religions. Then we'll exchange keywords later."

"Ok. What's the deadline?

"Monday. Twelve noon - on the dot!"

Saturday

I really ought to start working soon. We're all depending on each other – I can't let the others down.

The phone rings. It's Bert.

"Ready for some beach volleyball?"

"Sorry Bert, I've got to study."

"Oh, come on! It's boiling hot – you can study later on this evening."

"Is Martin coming?"

"No."

Tired and sunburnt, I go to bed without having read a single word about Roman religion.

Sunday

I'm lying on my back, looking at the sky and dreaming about holidays. John comes up to the loft.

"We've been given the topic for the exam. We've got to talk for ten minutes about two religions and the role of religious specialists."

"What do you mean by religious specialists?"

"Priests, mainly. The exam goes like this: first, we have to do our presentation and then the examiners will ask topical questions about the religions for twenty minutes."

Monday

For four hours I sit tapping on the keyboard, making keywords. At noon I click 'send' and my e-mail flies off to Helena and John. Ben, my engineering-student housemate, saunters into the living room.

"Do your memory techniques work, Oddbjørn?"

"I've only made keywords about Roman religions so far. Before I can start using Memo, I need John and Helena's notes. They've got the notes on 80 percent of the syllabus."

"The exam's on Wednesday. Are you going to memorise everything in two days?"

"Yes."

"With no prior knowledge and no lectures? Just two days' study?"

There's hardly a soul in the library. Why am I doing this to myself, I could be playing beach volleyball? I get out my mobile phone and step out into the hall to call Bert. Pull yourself together, Oddbjørn! All you need is to use Memo and it'll be done in a flash! Prove to Martin how effective it is! I decide against calling Bert. After two rings, I hang up.

The notes for my presentation cover just two pages. Memorising them is a breeze. After a quick lunch, I've memorised two more religions.

"I want to teach you the memory technique, John. It works great."

"I doubt I've got time."

"It's quick to learn and easy to use."

"I've always been sceptical about stuff like that – all the knowledge just goes in one ear and out the other."

"There's every reason to be sceptical, but this isn't the same thing as traditional memorising, maps of keywords or rote learning. Memo, my technique, connects the knowledge to your long-term memory. You'll remember it for months. For years, if you practice a bit."

"What's Memo really about?"

"In short, you visualise keywords in locations you are familiar with. Places that are already a part of your long-term memory. You always know where to look for the knowledge you need and you can easily retrieve it."

"Maybe next time. Let's see how you do first."

Tuesday

By dinnertime I've memorised what I need about Greek and Roman religions. Quite funny, really, as the Greeks and Romans used similar techniques back in ancient times. Ben listens to me practice my presentation after dinner.

"Why are you doing this?" Ben asks.

"I already know that the knowledge I acquire using this method remains in place for a long time, but I want to see how quickly I can acquire that knowledge. And it's a motivating way of learning new things. After learning to remember, I thirst for knowledge!"

"Have you memorised a lot for that exam on religions?"

"Yes, but I still don't know anything about Norse mythology or Mesopotamian religions."

Ben laughs. "And the exam's tomorrow?"

"One o'clock. I'll have to get up at the crack of dawn," I say, looking at the use-by date on the coffee.

Wednesday

My alarm clock has let me down; two whole religions to memorise in just a few hours. At noon I meet John by the church. We go to the examination room. John points at the notice board.

"We're supposed to go in at the same time; different examiners. Half past two."

"Great, then we've got time for some revision."

"That Greek creation myth is pretty interesting," John says.

"What? I haven't read anything about that," I reply, heading to the toilet.

Back from the toilet, John tells me I'm now going in at two.

"Someone didn't show up."

"Five minutes left, then. Can I have your notes on the creation myth?"

Zeus, Cronus, Uranus. Thank god for Memo.

"Next candidate is Oddbjørn By," the secretary announces.

I enter the room. The two examiners - a bespectacled old man and a lady with a big smile - stand up.

"I know we're allowed to bring in a page of keywords for the presentation, but the Greeks and Romans really valued memory. Speaking freely from memory was considered a virtue. That's also how I want to do my presentation."

The examiners look baffled, but perhaps that is the point?

"In India the priests memorised the *Rig Veda*, a religious work, as they were afraid that any incorrect citing of the story would cause cosmic imbalance. That is why the current version is very similar to the original. Similarly, the Egyptians feared cosmic imbalance if they did not worship their gods," I say and begin my presentation on the Egyptian and Roman priesthoods.

The introduction gives me a real kick. The clock is ticking and I do my stuff for ten minutes. Bang, bang, bang. Twelve seconds over time the lady stops me.

"Tell me about the sources of Sámi religion," the man says.

I'm well acquainted with the ruins of the old brewery. This is where I visualised the keywords about the Sámi religion. I travel back in my mind and pick out the keywords I want to use to answer.

Memo works perfectly. The keywords I've memorised are easy to retrieve and expand upon. The man asks whether I've read Edward what's-his-name's book. Oh no, I've never heard of him! I'm going to fail! The man lifts his hand and smiles.

"That's OK," he says. "It's not on the reading list."

The lady takes over and tests me on Greek religion.

I dole out the knowledge I've acquired over the past 48 hours. She gets me on a question about the Oracle. There was nothing in my notes about the inscription over the door in Delphi. Time's up. I shake the examiners hands and smile.

At half past four I cycle over to the notice board. A bunch of students are discussing the marks.

"Average was a C," says a girl.

I note my grade and get back on my bike.

"How did you do?" asks the girl.

"Aced it" I reply, blushing slightly.

Summer passed. In August I met Martin again. I told him about the exam.

"How would you do if you sat the exam again now?" Martin asks.

"It's easy to refresh your knowledge using Memo, so if I had three hours or so to revise, I could get a distinction at least."

Martin smiles.

"One day you should write a book, Oddbjørn. To teach others how you do it."

How to read this book

Your brain is your greatest asset. Your mind and memory is your toolbox, and, just like a builder, your mind uses different tools to effectively do different tasks. This book teaches you how to use the different memory techniques, so you won't have to use the hammer all the time. Each tool will help your memory become more effective.

To get the most out of this book, you should start by reading *How your memory works*. This chapter contains the basics - the whole book is, by and large, based on this chapter. Following this is a chapter on numerical systems. You don't need to learn these the first time you read the book, but I recommend that you have a look through, as several later chapters refer to the numerical systems. Let the book be your hardware store, where you go and pick up the tools you need, when you need them.

In this book I reveal the method, called Memo, which I use to memorise for exams, for everyday situations and in competitions. You will learn how to store anything you may want or need to remember, so you can easily retrieve it whenever you need to. People who participate in memory competitions are not unbelievably good at recalling information - they are good at memorising information. They can easily retrieve the information, as they have stored it systematically. It is these methods this book will teach you. So far, tens of thousands of people in Norway have used this book to improve their memory. Now it is your turn.

Unfortunately there are lots of ineffective memory books on the market, which have caused unnecessary confusion and scepticism. In addition, many of the books' authors conceal their very best memory techniques, as if they are afraid of losing in memory competitions. If you have heard about memory techniques before, you have probably heard that you are supposed to make maps of your keywords, or stories about what you want to remember. Many readers think memory books are a waste of time as they feel the techniques are tiresome and complicated. I understand this point of view as there are better and easier methods you can use to remember things.

Personally, I have continued to get good marks in exams after even shorter study periods. More importantly: lots of other people have learned to use Memo and they too have achieved excellent marks on exams. An exam is often a test of memory and I have achieved good marks by managing to quickly and correctly retrieve the information I have acquired. I could retrieve it so easily because I knew where I had stored it.

Not long after the book was published in Norway in 2006, this email, from an opera singer, popped up in my mailbox:

> "Last autumn I prepared for a role as Leonora in *Trovatore* by Verdi. Forty-five minutes of effective singing – and it took over a month to learn it all. Ideally I learn it all BEFORE the rehearsals, as this helps relax the muscles and reinforce the lyrics and melodies."

I told her to try Memo, gave her a few extra hints (all included in this edition) and waited for her reply. A few weeks later I received another email from the opera singer:

> "I am now preparing for my role as Desdemona in *Othello* by Verdi. I started to learn it ten days ago and I am finished. The role is fifty

minutes of effective singing, so I am satisfied. PS: It is really a superb book."

The purpose of this book is not to make you stop using memory aids and start memorising your shopping lists. The purpose is to teach you the tools you need so you can remember what you *want* to remember.

A word of caution: Memo is not a system that will just copy knowledge into you memory. No memory technique can do that. Remembering a thousand decimals of pi or the entire syllabus for an exam is not easy, but Memo is the easiest way. What you want to remember still has to come from somewhere – lectures, books, conversations. Memo is about spending less time learning and remembering and more time doing other things. In this book you can find the tools you need to remember everything from names to first aid and decks of cards to foreign languages. The most important techniques take just a few minutes to learn and are easy to use. You will learn to store information in your long-term memory – no more forgetting exam notes or lyrics a week later.

How your memory works

We easily remember things we are passionate about. You probably have a super memory in certain areas. Some people remember an awful lot about tractors; others remember football results, bridge parties or celebrity gossip. The most important reason we remember details like these is that we put this knowledge into a wider context, either consciously or unconsciously. Most people are interested in remembering names, facts for exams or telephone numbers, but these can be more difficult to remember than trivial facts we are genuinely interested in. In this book, you will learn to place the knowledge you want to remember in context and into a system. Before we look at the powerful techniques we will use to remember things, we will go through four elements essential to improving the memory: observation, association, visualisation and location. These elements are the fundamentals of the memory.

Observation

Leonardo da Vinci once said "All knowledge has its origin in our senses." He was so observant that he could portray how birds take off, in detail, several hundred years before photos could prove him correct. You need not be as observant as Leonardo. The point is that your chance of remembering things increases if you watch what's going on. IQ tests often include a test where you look at a picture for a few seconds, only to be asked later about what was in the picture. Many people think this is a test of 'photographic' memory, but such tests are actually about testing your observation skills. You cannot possibly remember the colour of the shoes if you didn't observe them. If you did observe the colour of the shoes, you would probably remember the answer. If you looked at the shoes and forgot the colour, it was probably because you were not observing consciously.

Association

Observation itself is often not enough. You can look through a deck of cards without remembering the order. One reason for this may be that the cards don't mean anything to you. You need a system to organise your knowledge. Try not to think of a horse. No, don't think about a horse. Horse, horse, horse. What happened? You thought about a horse, of course. Because we have learnt that this hoofed-animal, of the species *Equus*, used for riding and pulling things, is called a "horse". Whenever we read or hear the word, we see the animal in our mind, even though the word "horse" really does not have anything to do with the animal. The word is just an association we have created for this type of animal.

The trouble with remembering numbers is that we cannot imagine numbers in the same way as words. No picture pops up when you hear the numbers 138 or 84739. I can ask you not to think about the number 309381084739and you have probably forgotten it already. One reason for this is that you cannot imagine it. To remember long strings of figures or other abstract concepts, we have to make associations that we can use to visualise. I have fixed associations for numbers. When I see the number 86, I think of Al Capone. Always.

Association can be defined as the connection between two or more thoughts or impressions so that one easily draws the other to mind. If I say "Calvin", you may think "Klein". In this book you will learn to acquire knowledge using associations. When you encounter texts, foreign languages, facts for exams, or names, you are really testing your ability to create associations. You often have to make up the associations yourself, something you are already a master of. You make associations all day long: you associate bacon with eggs and the sound of bells may remind you of the ice cream van.

Visualisation

Visualisation is imagination. To remember things more easily, we should make our information as visual as possible. That is why I would rather imagine Simon Crean arresting someone than remember the number 5684. Later in the book you will see how I transposed the number 5684 to a picture of Simon Crean. This book is about a lot more than just remembering numbers. You will learn to turn all sorts of information into lively pictures so that your chances of remembering them increase. Visualising, instead of just thinking, is a powerful technique. When combined with location, visualisation is the most important element in Memo.

Location

"Location, location, location!" As real estate agents say, location is everything. You can associate and visualise as much as you want, but without using locations, you risk losing a lot of the information. All top competitors at the World Memory Championships use a kind of location, meaning that they visualise what they need to remember in places they are familiar with. Location is the most powerful memory technique you will ever learn. Until now, all memory training has focused too much on how to remember better. But how you remember information is unimportant. It is where and how you store the information that is so vital. You have the knowledge in your mind somewhere, but where are you supposed to look for it?

Journeys

Do you ever get lost on the way to work and end up arriving four hours late? Of course not. Because you know the way.

A journey is about location and is the most powerful memory technique. The technique is not very widely known, although it was used a great deal by the Greeks and Romans of ancient times. Paradoxically, it seems to have been forgotten since. The journey method is based on thinking of a journey through a familiar landscape. Houses and other clearly defined spaces are very effective. Along the journey, you define - places where you can store the information to be used later.

Think of your house or the house you grew up in. Start outside the front door. This is the first point. Go through the door to the second room - this is your second point. Decide on ten clearly defined locations throughout the house and write them down, or visualise the points without writing them down. The points should have a logical order, as it is easier to remember your journey that way. Go through walls and floors if that helps create more order. My journey looks like this:

1 – outside the front door	6 – study
2 – hallway	7 – bathroom
3 – stairs	8 – laundry
4 – kitchen	9 – bedroom
5 – living room	10 – sister's bedroom

Read through the list of ten points in your house until you are sure of the order. Put the list aside. Now we are going to go through ten words. The first word is *dam*. Visualise a dam at the first point - outside the front door. It's a good idea to imagine some ducks swimming in the dam, as movement can make the picture easier to remember. The next word you visualise at the second point - in the hallway. Each word is thus visualised at its own location, or room, along the journey - no matter how illogical it is to find the word in that location. Don't dwell for too long on each word but try to maintain an even rhythm. Here is the whole list:

1. Dam
2. Helicopter
3. Lithium Battery
4. Berries
5. Border Collie
6. Car
7. Knight
8. Ox
9. Flower
10. Neon sign

Quickly read through the list once more if you like. In a minute you will write down what you visualised at each point. If you have forgotten a word, don't dwell for too long, but go on to the next word. The word will probably pop up soon. Close the book and write down the words.

You have now memorised associations for the first ten elements in the periodic table. The names of the elements are hydrogen (a dam produces *hydro*electricity), helium (helicopter), lithium (modern batteries are called lithium batteries), beryllium (berry), boron (Border Collie), carbon (car), nitrogen (knight), oxygen (ox), fluorine (flower) and neon (neon sign). The reason we visualised a dam for hydrogen and a flower for fluorine is that these atoms are difficult to imagine. That is why I made associations that are easier to visualise. This is an important principle when memorising.

We can also add more information about the elements to the points in the journey, like the atomic weight and when the atom was discovered. We don't need to memorise the atomic number, as the point in the journey indicates the number of element. Oxygen is number eight and comes at the eighth location on the journey.

The way we remembered the words was special. We brought in the long-term memory - in this case the journey through the house. Then we stored the new knowledge straight in the long-term memory instead of in the more limited short-term memory.

Some people think journeys only give us more to remember, as we have to remember the journey and the information we memorised. But think about it: hundreds of journeys are already stored in your long-term memory. You just need to define the points. Using journeys to learn and remember new information is very useful. One reason journeys are so effective is that you must visualise the knowledge instead of just thinking about it.

One of Scandinavia's best memory people, Torgeir Farsund Thorrud, once said this about why location is so important: "Without location, you're just storing your knowledge in thin air. Locations function like a piece of paper, something you can write your knowledge on." If you were to remember the ten words above without Memo, you would just be writing them in thin air. The journey is the piece of paper you wrote them down on.

New tasks

I would like you to try a new task, no matter how the last one went. To avoid mixing it up with the last list, you should make up a new journey. The reason being that you will see the dam at the first point of that journey for quite a long time - maybe for weeks, even if you don't repeat the exercise. This demonstrates the strength of the system. If the list of the ten elements were knowledge you were supposed to remember forever, you would have had to repeat it occasionally. That is why you should wait a while before using the same journey again. This can be compared to daily experiences at actual places. Events you have experienced in one place don't get mixed up with new events, even though they occur at the same place. This means you can visualise new things in the same journey as long as you separate them in time. You should let your journeys rest for a few days before re-using them.

One advantage of using a journey is that it provides storage space for your knowledge. We separate information to avoid untidiness. If, for example, we'd stored all the words at the same location, chaos would have reigned. If you want to learn more than ten elements, you make a longer journey, or you can visualise two words at each point. Then one of the words will often give you a clue as to what the other word is. If the order is important, you should have a set rule for where you place the word. For example, the first word you place in the locations should always be at the top, at the bottom or to the left of the second word. But putting three or more words at the same location is counterproductive – the point of using the journey is to divide the information into smaller chunks to avoid confusion.

We'll now try memorising two words at one point. This time write down a new journey consisting of seven points from a house, shopping centre, the outdoors or work. If you forgot a word in the last exercise, try adding details or movement to try to remember better. You can also try to find logical reasons for the object you want to remember being at that very point on the journey. If the berries were in the kitchen in the last task, it was because you were having dessert. The associations for the elements in the periodic table were based on word plays like ox – oxygen. It is easier to memorise when you make up the associations yourself.

Here is a list of the fourteen largest countries in the world by area. To create the associations, you can use word plays or famous people, or items you associate with the country. The first thing that pops into your mind is usually the best. To make the association easy to memorise, it is important that it can be visualised – that you can see it in your mind. First, decide on associations for all countries. Then, memorise the list of associations you made - two associations at each location in the journey. It may be a good idea to place the first word to the left and the second to the right, as the order of the words is important in this task. Let's go!

Country	Association	Suggestion
Russia		Vladimir Putin
Canada		Maple leaf
USA		Mickey Mouse
China		Dragon
Brazil		Soccer ball
Australia		Kangaroo
India		Curry
Argentina		Maradona
Kazakhstan		Kazoo or Casserole
Sudan		Saddam
Algeria		Algae
Congo		Bongo (drums)
Saudi Arabia		Sultan
Mexico		Sombrero

Read quickly through the list once more. Close your book and write down what you can see at each point - now! How did you do? If you managed more than ten, that's fantastic! Well done to perform that well with a new method. If you forgot a word, don't worry. Usually you need time to repeat what you are learning for an exam. With practice the methods will become more efficient.

How much information to memorise at each point along the journey depends on the information you want to memorise. The safest thing is to visualise a few keywords at each point, typically

28

one or two. Too many details in one location may be difficult to recall. When you are memorising, you may forget what the association is supposed to represent. You may remember 'dam', but you have forgotten that the dam represents hydrogen. To avoid this problem, you can read what the association stands for once more.

To remember the words in the list permanently, you should repeat the list straightaway, preferably more than once. After that, repeat as and when necessary at progressively longer intervals. If you had memorised the list without using Memo, you might have remembered 5-6 countries and you probably wouldn't have remembered them in the correct order.

What can journeys be used for?

The journey method is perfect if you want to remember information in order. Anything from keywords in a best man's speech, a deck of cards, or the correct position for a guitar chord in a song can be memorised. Journeys also suit information whose order is irrelevant. I use Journeys to memorise different facts for exams and things I should do. As you can see, Memo isn't just about memorising decks of cards or shopping lists. Perhaps it took you 30 to 60 seconds to memorise the country list. Think about what an advantage Memo will give you when learning fifty keywords for an exam, a speech or the steps in first aid. Here is an example of how useful the journey method can be.

Dancing

I once did a salsa dancing course. As the boy has to lead, he is the one who has to remember all the steps. Learning the basic steps or combinations was no problem. The problem was remembering them when wanting to improvise. Often I did the same step over and over whilst desperately trying to remember more steps. It can be compared to sitting an exam: you already know quite a lot, but you don't always manage to recall all of it.

The solution was surprisingly successful. I wrote down the fourteen steps I knew and then I memorised them with the help of a journey. The first step, croqueta y paseala, I visualised at a woodwork bench in high school. I imagined a croquet mallet (an association for croqueta) being sawn up. The next move on was the sombrero. I visualise a sombrero on the woodwork bench. For the steps I did not know the name of, I made a suitable picture to remind me of the step. For example, I imagined a policeman to remind me of a step that begins with holding the girl's hands as if the police were arresting her. When dancing, it is important to be decisive. Knowing what the next steps are going to be, it is easy to be decisive. In the past, I would always get nervous, but now I can take the girl by the hand with confidence. While dancing, I can walk mentally from room to room in high school - easily recalling the steps Croqueta, sombrero, kentucky, setenta, variación and ochenta. At any time, I can leave my journey and improvise and then return and continue where I left off. Or start at chance points along my journey.

Instead of concentrating on finding steps, I can concentrate on the rhythm. I am sure to remember all the steps I know and get maximum use out of all the steps. When I learn new steps, I just memorise them along my journey - safely stored in my long-term memory.

I have also memorised moves for disco dancing, like John Travolta's moves in Pulp Fiction. It's good to have an extensive repertoire. Even with just twenty moves, you'll be rocking like never before! Improvisation is for pros and even pros plan their improvisations.

Remembering future events

"Why didn't you take out the rubbish?"

The journey method is a technique that entails recollecting things in the past, to store information you can later recall. On a daily basis we often forget things to do in the future: we forget to post letters, call the boss or lock the door.

In the chapter entitled *Profiles and records* you can read about great memory masters. The thrice world champion, Andi Bell, taught me a good method for remembering daily tasks. Whenever he lies in bed and gets a good idea, he can't be bothered to find paper. He only thinks about the idea and chucks his pen on the floor. When he sees the pen the next morning, it reminds him of the idea. If Andi had just put the pen on the desk, he probably wouldn't have remembered the idea, but the very fact that the pen is in an unusual spot is the thing that gets us to remember the idea.

You throw your clothes into the washing machine, but forget to take them out. Forgetting them may, in part, be explained by the old proverb 'out of sight, out of mind'. But if we use Andi's tip we can use an object to remind us of the clothes in the washing machine. Put an orange on the bed and think of the washing and you'll remember to hang the clothes out to dry before you go to bed. I like to call this technique the *orange method,* because an orange on the bed or the floor draws your attention. But you don't have to use oranges – anything in an unusual place will do.

You can also create other hints to aid your memory by moving things. For example, you get up at 7 am and remember it's your brother's birthday, but it's too early to call him. To ensure you phone him later that day, place your bed at an unusual angle. Home from work you see the bed in a peculiar position and call to say happy birthday. Try for yourself and see how effective this method is.

Do you ever forget to brush your teeth before you go to bed? Hardly – the routine is so ingrained that it will be hard to forget. Let's pretend that you have to remember to lock an important door before you go to bed. To remember, you can tie it to the tooth brushing routine. Put your toothbrush in the bathroom cabinet. Place something unusual in front of it, perhaps your boyfriend's special hair-regrowth shampoo. When you go to brush your teeth you cannot get to it without noticing the shampoo. The shampoo is the hint that tells you to lock the door – lock it before you brush your teeth so you won't forget. Take the shampoo with you and don't let go of it until the door is locked.

The advantage of placing the toothbrush in the cabinet, with the shampoo in front of it, is that you will only see the hint when you need it. If you had left the shampoo on the hand basin you would have got used to seeing it during the day and ignored it in the evening. The shampoo bottle may be too big for the cabinet, but you will think of something smart. At work you can place your jacket under a cup or something like that if you have a tendency to forget to turn on the alarm before you leave. Unless you tend to forget your jacket too!

Sometimes it's a good idea to write down what you want to remember. But you don't always have a pen at hand. You're surfing the Internet and a friend calls and asks whether you're coming over later. He wants you to return the movie you borrowed. You write 'remember DVD' on a post-it and carry on surfing. You might remember the film, you might not. For the note to work, you have to see it before you go out. But as you already have a visual hint, the DVD, the easy way is to put the DVD in a place you will pass before you go out. Put the movie in the hallway or on top of your shoes. Do it now, while you still remember to do it.

Of course, the orange method will cause chaos if you live with a lot of people. But you can always put the orange on your chair, desk or hang a sock on the door handle. Anything can be put anywhere in your field of vision to remember what you're supposed to, as long as it's in an unusual enough place. Leave my book lying around the house so you remember to read it.

Four challenges for the future

Here are four challenges for your memory: You have to take vitamins every day, remember to bring your umbrella home with you, ring the bank and post letters on the way home from work. Some of the solutions may sound obvious, while others may be new to you.

Taking your vitamins everyday involves two challenges: actually remembering to take them and remembering whether or not you have taken them. To remember to take your vitamins you ought to make a hint to prevent the 'out of sight, out of mind' effect. As your aim is to take vitamins every day, you should make a routine. It's easier to remember to take them if you decide to take them with a particular meal. You can also use the technique of association. You eat cornflakes for breakfast everyday. Imagine the packet being full of vitamins until the routine becomes automatic. When you take out the packet of cornflakes every morning, it will remind you to take vitamins. The reason I decided not to associate the vitamins with the carton of milk is that I drink milk all the time, so I would start ignoring the association whenever I drank milk. I would end up ignoring the association when I really should be paying attention to it. You don't need to do anything drastic, but associating new routines with old ones is an effective technique which will help you remember ahead. To remember that you've taken your vitamins that day, you can simply turn the container on its head once you've taken them. But remembering whether you have taken vitamins today is a test of your memory in the past. You can learn more about that later in the book.

To not forget your umbrella, my advice is to use pairing. Pairing is a technique by which you physically pair unforgettable things with things that are easy to forget. For example, when you put your umbrella down at other people's houses, you should hang it on your jacket instead of on a peg, because you'll need the jacket when you leave. You probably won't forget your jacket and then you've only got one thing to remember because the umbrella is hanging on your jacket. If the umbrella is dry, you can put it in your shoe or in the arm of your jacket. But if you hang your umbrella on a peg, you've got two things to remember. If you also put your gloves and scarf in the pocket and hang the umbrella on the jacket, you've only got one load to remember, not four.

That some tasks are time specific can both help and challenge your memory. You chuck a pizza in the oven. Remembering to take it out again is easy – you set the timer. Remembering to call the bank is easy if you have agreed to ring at 2 o'clock - you can just set the alarm on your mobile phone. But if you've agreed to ring at any time, you may just end up putting it off indefinitely and forget the whole thing. The solution is to do it straight away, while you are consciously thinking about it, or set an alarm for a suitable time.

Your fourth challenge is to post letters on the way home from work. Why do we forget such things? One reason might be that you get distracted at the very moment you were supposed to be focusing on posting those letters. If you see the post box, the chances of remembering to post the letters increase, but manipulating your attention in the right direction at the right time is difficult. One way to increase your chances is to visualise what you are supposed to do beforehand. Imagining what you're supposed to do is a powerful technique that you probably use already, either consciously or unconsciously. One variation on this is to imagine someone else doing the same thing. Imagine Donald Duck posting the letter, walking to the chemists and doing other tasks you need to do. The advantage is that you can search for Donald in your mind and immediately see what he is doing. After you've memorised many tasks, you can swap Donald for other figures to avoid confusion.

Just blaming your memory when you forget tasks is wrong. Your attentiveness is the real culprit. Visualisation guarantees nothing, but it is of great help.

Memory aids

The use of memory aids is another technique that you can use for the past and future. It is also based on the 'out of sight, out of mind' principle. If you are supposed to collect a book, you should construct a hint you will see. If you don't see it, you risk the task slipping out of your mind, but of course this depends on the situation. In fact, you can remember things by putting a little blank note in your line of vision. If you write what you are supposed to do on the note, you specify what it is you ought to remember.

Often it's a good idea to write lists of things you need to remember to free your thoughts. Journeys function the same way, as you are 'writing' down what you want to remember along the journey. You concentrate for a moment to memorise what you need and then you can free your thoughts for other things. When I am memorising for exams, I 'write' keywords along my journeys. I store my knowledge in the journeys and can retrieve it when I please. The only thing I need to remember is where I have stored that knowledge. If I have memorised it properly, it's easy to retrieve. I don't need to worry about forgetting it and I am much less nervous about the exam than I was in the past.

Summary

Journey method

- Use the orange method
- Make your task visible to avoid the 'out of sight, out of mind' effect
- Move things into unusual positions to make hints
- Establish routines
- Link new routines to old ones
- Visualise
- Use an alarm
- Do it now, if you can
- Use pairing

Here, there and everywhere

Do you remember which day of the week Christmas Eve 1989 fell on? What about 31 August 1997 – which day of the week was that? 31 August 1997 may be easier to work out when you know this was the day Princess Diana died. Remembering weekdays for random dates is difficult – there is no logic to it. But people are good at remembering details from special days, like the day Diana died. Which day of the week was 11 September 2001? Think about it.

Our sense of place or location is especially strong in our memory. You may not remember that 31 August 1997 was a Sunday, or that 11 September was a Tuesday, but it is almost guaranteed that you remember where you were when you saw the news on TV or were told about it.

Humans are really good at remembering the layout of houses. Often we can walk through a house once and remember the layout for years. We can remember for months who sat around the table at a particular restaurant or a corporate lunch. Remembering who sat where for dinner at home can be harder, as it is easily mixed with prior dinners.

What did you do today? Our answers are often centred on where we were. "I had breakfast, stopped by the petrol station, went to work, picked up a package at the post office, and went to the gym." It is all about the location of what we did. Some police forces have introduced new interrogation methods that are designed to take advantage of this. To illustrate the technique I'll ask you to think about your bedroom. Describe it as well as you can, with all its details. To get better witness statements the police try to get the witness to take a more active part. They do this by asking questions like: Your back is facing the window, what do you see? Look up, what's on the ceiling? Imagine that you are standing by the bed and bend over, what do you see? On average this interrogation method improves recall of information by over 40% compared with earlier methods.

Here is a test for you to try: come up with as many animals as you can in one minute. And no, a duck is not considered to be an animal. A duck is a bird and salmon is a fish. Include a friend in the task, or write down as many as possible now.

The animal test is to test what is called semantic memory. Semantic memory is a part of the long-term memory that stores general knowledge. Informal tests with friends usually result in 18 to 25 animals. It can be quite fun to see how many vegetables or animals you can come up with in one minute.

The test has nothing to do with Memo. But other tasks can show the difference in remembering with and without Memo, in normal, healthy people. Doctors sometimes test semantic memory by giving the patient sixteen pictures to remember, then asking them to recall them. In another test twenty words are read out several times, in order, up to five times. Afterwards you are asked to recall as many as possible. Doctors say that it is "very unlikely that you will remember them all." Using the normally poor results from these tests as a reference point, you can already see how well you are doing, remembering the first ten elements of the periodic table having only read through the list once or twice.

Older people don't necessarily suffer from memory loss if they can still recall what they did yesterday. If they can also add detailed examples of when their memory actually lets them down, then it's unlikely that they suffer from a memory related illness. If they cannot recognise a $100 note, however, it might be time to visit the doctor. The test is based on showing a person something new or something that has recently been changed. The person is asked: "which note is this?" As people with dementia struggle to learn new things, few the dementia patients will recognise the note (Wetterberg, 2005).

Most of the methods in this book are based on a visual mindset. I was therefore a bit nervous when I held a seminar for newly blind people in late 2006. Having taught them the journey method, I read out ten words. Almost all of them remembered the words and the correct order. Next they quickly learned the ten largest countries in the world, by area.

One of the guys at the seminar was born blind, but he still managed to memorise them all perfectly. He recalled it all perfectly both backwards and forwards. He obviously has an image in his mind for what an ox or helicopter looks like, even if he has never seen one.

Hopefully you will find many situations where you can use Memo. You don't have to stop writing down your shopping list and start memorising it, but at least you know how to memorise bread and milk should the need arise. Use the tips in this book when you are giving a presentation or sitting an exam. At least your memory will not be the obstacle!

Numerical Systems

There are numbers all around us. In many instances it is advantageous to have a predetermined system to use when memorising numbers. In this chapter you will find the four systems I use for memorising numbers, depending on the purpose and complexity of the task: the Single System; the Double System; the Alternative Double System; and the Triple System. You don't have to learn them all, but read through the systems to get an overview. Later you can learn them all or just those that are most suitable to you. I am convinced that you will find good uses for the systems –to remember pin-numbers, dates, phone numbers or simply the numbers you encounter on a daily basis.

The Single System

The simplest system is called the Single System. In this system we create one figure for each number. We could also call it the simple system. Learning this system is a good investment, as it has many useful applications. As we were not created to remember numbers, we must attach something more meaningful to them. For example, you could associate a ball or an egg with the number zero.

- 1 looks like a pencil or a flagpole.
- A swan is the perfect symbol for the number 2.
- The number 3 could be handcuffs.
- 4 looks like a sailboat.

- The number 5 is tougher, but with a little bit of imagination it looks like a hook. Like Captain Hook in Peter Pan. Or maybe a sea horse?
- 6 looks like an elephant's trunk, or an old-fashioned push lawnmower.
- 7 could be a boomerang or a diving board.
- A Snowman, or an hourglass works perfectly for number 8. Jennifer Lopez could also works.
- When you get to 9, what about an axe or a balloon?

Decide on an association for each number – feel free to create your own. If Santa Claus makes you think of the number 4, use that. The main thing is to link the number to the image. Even more importantly, you must be able to visualise - touch physically - the associations you choose (that's why numbers are hard: they are abstract). To learn your associations properly, you must repeat them occasionally. This goes for the other numerical systems too.

The Single System has many uses. It is perfect for remembering anything from house numbers and time to pin numbers and passwords. To memorise the four-digit code 8364 you can use a journey with four points. Visualise the association for one number at each point. The journey will tell you the order, the association the number. This is a quick and simple way to remember numbers. The Single System, however, has its limitations, as it does not reduce the amount of information you have to memorise. Later you can read about the optimum ways to memorise codes, passwords and more.

Try to memorise sixteen numbers using the Single System. Think of a journey consisting of eight separate points and visualise two associations at each point: 1415926535897932.

When dealing with long numbers, the journeys and stories can get too long and the snowman will show up often enough to create confusion. In cases like this, the double or Triple System is much easier. The Single System is, however, elementary and often used to supplement the double systems. And congratulations – you now know the first sixteen decimals of pi! In the Single System we get one association per number. The Double System divides the numbers into pairs; a combination of the double and Single Systems is therefore ideal for memorising three and five-digit numbers and longer odd numbers.

The Double System

As the name indicates, the Double System is based on dividing the numbers into chunks of two digits. 10 could be Maradona, as that was his number when he played soccer. 07 could be James Bond and 99 Wayne Gretzky, the Canadian hockey player. Numbers are much easier to remember as visual associations. The challenge is to create one hundred associations. The numbers are translated into letters - the system is essentially a translation program.

Using the Double System, the numbers are first divided into pairs and then translated using this formula:

1 = N   Number oNe

2 = T   Two

3 = B   3 looks like B

4 = R   R looks like a mirror-image 4, with an extra line

5 = S   5 looks like S

6 = K   6 looks a little like a K

7 = L   7 is an upside down L

8 = M   The Mighty (Meighty) M

9 = g   9 looks like g

0 = F   because 0 is the final number

Only the consonants have a value. To create words we add vowels. 39 becomes Bg. Add an a and we get BaG. 21 is TN. TN can be turned into TeNt. 78 become LM. Add letters and we get LeMon. Even if lemon has another consonant after M, we only care about the first two. Always. We are only trying to remember two digits at a time. The words Cab and Brick can be translated back to C and B, the first two (and only) consonants in cab= 63. B and R are the first two consonants = 34.

Number			Association
32	B	T	BaT
33	B	B	BaBy
34	B	R	BRick
35	B	S	BuS
36	B	K	BucK
37	B	L	BaLL

Look in the appendix for suggestions for all hundred associations.

The point of an effective mnemonic system is to reduce information and consciously save it. Learning the Double System is a bit like writing an SMS. You may hit the wrong buttons to begin with, but it soon becomes automatic. You don't have to learn hundred associations in one go to; learn the basics and use the appendix to look up specific numbers you may need in a speech, an exam or an interview. Use Memo to translate boring numbers into fascinating images. Now you are on your way to learning how to remember phone numbers, pin numbers, birthdays and much more.

The Alternative Double System (ADS)

507846379115

A soldier lassoing. Russel Crowe is melting. A giraffe is fishing.

As the name indicates, this is an alternative to the Double System. Unlike the Double System, you create associations based on *people* and *actions,* rather than *words.* The ADS was essentially created by the English memory pioneer Dominic O'Brien and is ideal for memorising cards or lots of numbers.

Dominic created a system where he made up set associations by translating each number into letters. The number zero looks like the letter o and 7 looks like an upside down L. The association for 07 could be O for Osama and L for Laden - Osama bin Laden. As a Norwegian I use other letters. But after a lot of testing I have found that the letters that Andi Bell, a British memory expert, use works best. This is how you can translate the numbers into letters to use for the people and the actions:

0 = O   because 0 looks like o

1 = i   1 looks like i

2 = t   Two

3 = E   3 looks like E

4 = R   R looks like a mirror-image 4, with an extra line

5 = S   5 looks like S

6 = C   6 looks like C

7 = L   7 is an upside down L

8 = A   8 looks a bit like A

9 = g   9 is similar to g

Should you forget how the letters are translated back into numbers, you can simply think of oitersclag, the order of the letters in the list above. Creating your own version of the translation may work better for you. For instance, the number 0 could be the letter D if you prefer that. You may prefer to create your own people and actions as associations. Those you make yourself are often easiest to remember. James Bond is a good association for 07. The associations will, eventually, become automatic regardless of which letters or associations you decide to use. The system of translation is made as easy as possible to simplify the learning of one hundred associations.

Here are some examples to show you how numbers are translated into letters and then into an association with a person or creature and an action:

			Person	**Action**
49	R	g	Rugby player	Rugging
50	S	O	Soldier	Soap
51	S	I	Sikh	Sit
52	S	T	Starfish	Stab

The number 5250 would give 'starfish soaping itself'.

In total we create one hundred associations of people or creatures with their accompanying actions, for the numbers 00 to 99. A complete list of suggestions is found in the appendix.

Lets have another look at the numbers at the beginning of this chapter: 507846379115. The first four digits become a soldier lassoing. The next four become Russell Crowe melting. If you have to remember the numbers for a long time, you should store them in a journey, or, as an alternative, somewhere you feel it is natural to look for them. I have found that this is where most memory improvement books come up short: they don't tell you how to save the images, the associations. Imagining a soldier lassoing is not enough if you have a lot of numbers to remember - the image will end up floating around alongside other random information. To remember long strings of numbers we combine the system with journeys. The number at the start of the chapter could, for example, be stored on the way to the mailbox: The soldier lassoing on the doorstep. Russell Crowe melting in the garden. A giraffe fishing on the road. To recall the numbers, you just walk to the mailbox in your mind and look at the people you meet.

The Triple System

The last numerical system is called the Triple System. Ben Pridmore, a memory world champion, developed the Triple System at the start of this millennium. The rules for the Triple System are similar to those of the Double System; it is essentially a translation program from numbers to letters. The Double System is a derivative of the Triple System, with the difference being that we divide numbers into groups of three digits in the Triple System and, in addition to the consonants, the first vowel sound in the word also has a value.

In the Triple System, the first and third digits are always translated into a consonant. The second digit is always translated into a vowel. Therefore, each number has both a consonant and a vowel value.

Here are some suggestions for consonants for the Triple System:

1 = N	Number oNe
2 = t	Two
3 = B	3 looks like B
4 = R	R looks like a mirror-image 4, with an extra line

5 = S	5 looks like S
6 = K or C	6 looks a little like a C, but K is easier to use
7 = L	7 is an upside down L
8 = M	The Mighty (Meighty) M
9 = g or j	9 looks like g. J is an alternative letter to make it easier to create words
0 = F or TH	F because 0 is the final number. TH is an alternative

to make it easier to create words

The second digit in each three-digit group, or triple, is always translated into a vowel sound. As we don't have ten vowels in the alphabet, we have to base the system on vowel sounds. So we let the vowel symbolise the pronunciation, not the spelling.

Here are suggestions for vowel sounds for the Triple System:

1 = 'a' as in cat
2 = 'e' as in pet
3 = 'i' as in kitten
4 = 'o' as in tom
5 = 'u' as in puss
6 = 'A' as in hay
7 = 'E' as in bee
8 = 'I' as in high
9 = 'O' as in low
0 = 'oo' as in pool

Notice that the vowel sounds for 1 to 5 are in alphabetical order: a, e, i, o, u. The same order is then repeated for 6 to 9 to 0. The consonant for 6 is K, but you can use words starting with C as long as the pronunciation is a K-sound. 9 can be either g or j. It's easier to make words that way. 966, for example, become *gak*, but if you use the alternative letters you get *Jack*. Remember the first and third digits are always consonants and the second digit always a vowel sound. *It will always be consonant + vowel + consonant.* Hence, we get a picture simply by translating the number. 092 is foot. 649 is cog. 812 is mat. Now it is time for you to try one yourself. Start with 314. Try 872.

What about 3 digit combinations that don't automatically create three letter words using the consonant + vowel + consonant system? 731 become lin. But lin is not a word, so we add letters at the end until we get a word. Add a t or an e and we get lint, or line. Remember that only the first three letters count as the association for the number. Try a few more: do you know anyone that may answer to the name 136? Do you like meat (meet = 872)? 314 become Bar, 136 can be Nick.

The Triple System requires more time to master, but it will be worth it if you need a tool to remember lots of numbers. For day-to-day memory needs, the Single System and either the Double System or the ADS will serve your needs well. However, mastering the principles of the Triple System is still a worthwhile investment. The more you practice the faster you will become at creating on-the-spot associations when you need them, or you could spend some time creating and learning set associations for every number from 000 to 999. For memory competitions contestants mostly use the ADS or Triple System. The Alternative Double System seems to give the best results in competitions. You may have noticed that I have suggested using different letters in the translations for the Alternative Double System and the Triple System. This does not seem to be a disadvantage, but you can easily synchronise the systems by using the consonants from the Triple System in the ADS, instead of the letters oitersclag. To learn more about the Triple System, continue reading, or move on to the next chapter.

343 become Bob - Bob the Builder. Remember that the vowel symbolises the pronunciation, not the spelling. Some combinations are impossible to create words from. For example, 434 become rir. But I cannot find a celebrity or a word starting with rir. To get around this we simply invent an association with the sound of the letter, or invent a new word. For example, when I see rir, it makes me think of a giant construction crane. For no reason, I just do. But it has now become my association for remembering 434. Use people as associations for the numbers if that works. 761 become L a n – for example Langer (Justin). 831 becomes M i n, like (Kylie) Minogue. Or you can find associations in foreign languages.

Mastering the Triple System brings several advantages; most importantly we have fewer images to remember when we memorise. Using the Single System we create an image for each digit: the number 412546 becomes a sailboat, a pole, a swan, a hook, a sailboat and an elephant. In the Triple System we only have two three-digit sets: 412 and 546. When dealing with a number not divisible by three (e.g. 412 546 82) we supplement with the Single or Double Systems.

Occasionally, alternative letters may be used to make it easier to create words. The consonant p can be used instead of B when 3 is the third digit. Feel free to add your personal touch to make the system complete.

As a peg system

You may have heard about the 'peg system', also known as the 'the major system'. The peg system is somewhat similar to the Triple System, as it divides numbers into groups of three and is often used by students and a small number of memory competitors. One of the disadvantages with this system is that it only translates numbers into consonants. You then have to add vowels to create a word. The number 397 becomes tgl using the peg-system - add vowels and you get toggle. Creating words from 000 to 999 becomes more difficult. On the other hand, the Triple System translates 397 directly into tool.

The Double and Triple Systems can be used as sort of a peg system too, like a journey. To remember thirty keywords for a speech, you can hang each word on a peg in the Double System. The first three keywords you may want to remember for your Best-Man speech could be boat trip, police and broom.

The first keyword goes on the first peg, 01=FaN. Imagine an enormous fan lifting the boat. The next keyword goes on the next peg, 02 = FooT. Imagine a policeman licking his foot. Broom is the third keyword. The third peg is 03 = FaBric. Visualise the broom dancing in a fabric. When the time comes for you to recall the keywords, you think about the pegs in the system. Fan, foot and fabric. To remember the keywords you just think about what each of them are doing.

A lot of memory improvement books focus on the peg method and ignore journeys. But the peg method has significant limitations, like limited storage capacity. Use the pegs more than once and you create confusion and disorder. Until the fan puts the boat back down and disappears from your memory, you may not have anywhere to store new information. I never use the peg system, but it may work for you.

Using Numerical Systems

Can numerical systems be used for more than just bank account numbers and phone numbers? Here are some examples of practical uses for the numerical systems.

Pin numbers and passwords

Without even knowing it, people use memory methods to remember their pin numbers. A TV-reporter once told me that to remember her VISA card pin number, she imagines a 70 year old chatting up a 30 year old. The cameraman said he used the same method to remember the pin number on his mobile. But he used the pin so infrequently that he could not remember his association when the phone ran out of battery. Three unsuccessful tries later, he was asked for several security, pin and puk codes. But what were they?

Both people use associations to remember their codes. It does not matter if you imagine a broccoli or a Chinese person to remember the code. Where and how you have stored the code is what matters. You have to know *where* to look for it. But by using associations we risk forgetting the code when it is not used for a while. Whether you need to remember one or ten pin numbers doesn't matter, neither does the complexity and ingenuity of the associations. The solution is location.

Our memory can be compared to a giant filing room. Associations give us a lot of images or stories for pin numbers and passwords, but they are just spread around on the floor. Even without associations, the codes are just clutter on the floor. Using locations, we file them away in an orderly system. Passwords and codes are saved in logical locations where we can easily retrieve them. We always know where the information is stored. One method to remember your ATM code is to use the actual card as the location. You can use the last four digits of the card number as your code - the hint is close by in case you forget the code. A more secure option is to try to find a pattern on the back or front of the card that reminds you of the code – a code you choose yourself or the one you were given by the bank. Think about the pattern a few times if you are not heading to the ATM straight away.

The mobile phone method

On a mobile phone keypad, each individual number also corresponds to several letters. Try to create a word from your card's pin number, based on the letters on the mobile. Without using the predictive text/dictionary function on you mobile, you would get the word *wasp* if you type in the code 9277. So far the word is just clutter in your mind, so it is necessary to store the word where it is easy to retrieve in case you forget the code. A logical location for the ATM code would be the local bank branch. Imagine a wasp in the bank. If you forget the code you just have to think, "where did I store it?" In the bank, of course. There you will see the wasp.

A word like wasp is better than a word like warp. Wasp is concrete and easy to imagine. You can find good words by typing the code as an SMS, with the dictionary/predictive text turned on. Some codes are impossible to create words from. That is when the figure method can come in handy.

The Figure Method

My VISA card pin number is 4892. To remember that we can imagine figures that look like the numbers. 4 looks like a sailboat, 8 a snowman, 9 an axe and 2 a swan. In the past, memory methods were based only on associations. But associations alone are risky, as you have not stored them anywhere in your memory. All the competitors in international memory competitions use a *location* to remember information. That is, they tie it to a concrete geographical location that they know. In this example too, you can think of the local bank branch. Imagine the branch being flooded, the water splashing up to your knees. You have to use a sailboat to get around. Halfway to the teller you meet a snowman. He is staggering towards you; someone struck him in the back with an axe. Over by the teller, a swan is floating around - it must be there for you to tie the boat to. Should you forget the pin number you can replay this bank scene in your mind.

Most people have more than one credit card. You can store the pin numbers in different branches of the bank. This way you remember which code belongs to which card. Alternatively, you can store one code at the teller and one in the ATM. Your cards may come in red, blue or black - use that to differentiate them. Perhaps there is a communist in the bank, being stung by those wasps.

The home phone is the location for my mobile phone pin number. A payphone or a phone shop are also suitable places to store it. Being conscious of where you store it is most important – you have to know where to look.

Internet passwords. What a mess! But you may already have an idea about what I about to suggest. My email password is stepladder. I simply imagine a stepladder in my mailbox. Don't bother trying to log on - all my passwords are fictional.

Multiplication and the times tables

Are you among the many who struggle with your times tables, like 8 x 7 and 7 x 7? I once struggled with these myself. Let us try doing 8 x 7, using the Single System for the numbers and the Double System for the answer. 8 is a snowman in the Single System, 7 a diving board. The answer is 56. In the Double System 5 = S and 6 = K. We get SacK. Imagine the snowman jumping of the diving board and straight into a sack. If you find the eight-times-table challenging, it can be smart to think creatively. Start by thinking about a snowman (8). He comes across the numbers in the Single System in a magical, ten-point, journey. The associations from the Double System tell us the answers.

The wind is ruffling the snowman's tree-branch arms. He walks past a pole (1 in the Single System). A mirror is dangling from the pole. The snowman stretches his neck and sees himself in the mirror (8 x 1 = 8). A swan (2) flies by. It's got nook in its beak (nook = 16 in the Double System, 2 x 8 = 16).

"Wow," says the Snowman and keeps wandering. He steps on something hard; a pair of handcuffs (3). They have caught a little tree (24).

The snowman has barely taken another step before he stumbles into a sailboat (4). A bat (32) is hanging from the mast. Time to get out of here. A hook (5) falls from the sky. The snowman bends down to pick it up, but his carrot nose falls into a raft (40). Furious, the snowman runs after the raft, but rams straight into an elephant (6). The Roman (48) riding the elephant is not happy either.

The snowman takes off running, but slips onto a diving board (7) and dives straight into the sack (56).

Once out of the sack, another snowman (8) floats by. He's got a corkscrew (64) in his chest. "I am glad not to be him, but I'm going down," he sighs.

Luckily a balloon (9) drifts past and the snowman grabs it. It lifts him, but he gets stuck on a lotus (72) flower.

He cries a snowflake, it is all over. He is hungry and gets the taste of Noodles (10) in his mouth; he realises he's having dinner with a mafia boss (80)

Summary

To remember a lot of numbers in the correct order, you need two systems: one to store the information, keeping it in the right order and one to make the numbers more visual. The best way to remember long numbers is to use journeys. To make the numbers more visual you have several options. The Single System is quick and easy to learn and works well for shorter numbers. The Alternative Double System takes quite a while to learn, but once you have mastered it, memorising numbers is like a walk in the park. The rules of the Triple System are easy to learn and one hundred decimals of pi are reduced to only thirty-three images.

Which system to use depends on the task, but if you know the basic principles for two or three systems, you will get a lot further than without a system. Soon, you will notice that you spend less time and effort remembering pin-codes, phone numbers, dates and facts.

Tips for memorising effectively

Listen carefully; I shall say this only once

In the past I had the attitude that "it doesn't matter if I have to read this article one more time to learn it". The problem? I was not fully focused on learning, as I knew I would get another chance. There is not always a second chance though. This type of attitude is not very good as the level of distraction is high – it is easy to daydream when you let it happen. When I hear numbers that I am going to memorise I need to be focused. There is only one chance to get it right. From numerous competitions I have noticed that I remember more when the numbers are read out in a quick and even rhythm. When we are trying to learn something we should therefore try to focus. You don't necessarily need to stress through a list of historical dates when you want to memorise them. Try to pay attention from the start, with the attitude "listen carefully; I shall say this only once." Repetition can be important, but if you memorise properly the first time, most of the job is done.

Repetition

An institute in Norway organises "revolutionary" seminars in the art of learning better. The organisers promise that the participants will learn a system of repetition and revision that will secure their knowledge forever. So what is the point of the free refreshment course within two years? There is a massive difference in the need for repetition in normal learning methods and memorising. Without Memo it is possible to look through a deck of cards hundreds of times without remembering the order of the cards. With Memo we can remember the entire deck, without repetition. Once you have learned the method you will probably remember the deck of cards for a couple of days. If you want to remember it for the next month or the rest of the year you must do some revision. Repetition takes two main forms. You can either observe the information again or you can go through the information in your mind. The first form of repetition involves physically looking through the deck of cards several times to reinforce the visualisation you have already done. The second form of repetition is to mentally go through the visualisation you have already done. These repetition methods can be used when memorising decks of cards and the same methods can be used for memorising other types of information.

Let us say that the list of ten elements in the chapter on journeys is something you wish to remember for years. To secure the knowledge you memorise the list the normal way. Repeat it straight away, by re-reading the list again and reinforcing the mental images you have visualised. Later, when necessary, you repeat the list mentally. Or re-read it. Mental repetition means thinking through your journey and what is stored at each point. Writing down or talking about the information is also a useful form of repetition. Quite often we do repetitions unconsciously. Every time you think about that goal you kicked you ensure that it will take much longer to forget.

Useless repetition

There is no magic formula for how often you should revise. Repetition is pointless if you are not focused or interested in the knowledge you are trying to acquire. You can revise a hundred times without remembering what you just saw. Do you know which note Banjo Paterson is on? $5? $10? $20? Which way is he facing? The note is right in front of you. You have seen it thousands of times – how can you forget? I don't blame you. What is the point in remembering this? The point is that you have to be focused when you are trying to remember the name of the guy you just met, or are trying to revise keywords you are using in a presentation. Banjo is on the ten-dollar note. He is facing to the left.

Concentration

The most demanding activity I have come across, in terms of concentration, is the memory event called *spoken numbers*. A computer reads one number per second. The competitors are trying to memorise as many as possible and recall them in the correct order. You receive points until your first mistake; should you remember a hundred numbers but make a mistake with the second you only get one point. It is a hard event because you have no control over the speed of the event and you have to concentrate the entire time. To win the event at international memory competitions you have to stay focused for at least 120 seconds. Memorising the most decks of cards in an hour to then recall them in less than two hours is obviously demanding – but here you can take a break when you feel like. In spoken numbers you cannot relax because each second you will hear a new number, translate it into an association, visualise it in a journey and prepare for the next number. So how do the competitors focus and manage to keep this deep state of concentration? I have no magic formula. Most important is what you do *before* you have to be focused. Your brain should be well rested. If I want to ruin my performance at an event I make sure I don't sleep the night before. But don't be afraid of a sleepless night before an exam. Even if you are dead tired Memo will help you remember – it will just take longer.

Struggling to concentrate can be due to three factors. Your brain is tired, your body is tired, or you have consumed the wrong type of food or drink (or too much/not enough food or drink). You will notice your body getting tired before you notice that the brain is tired, but the brain needs rest too. To keep your concentration up you have to be focused when you memorise. Do not let other thoughts get in the way. Individuals who speed read tend to retain and remember more of what they have read because they must be focused. The same goes for memorising. Be effective when memorising and take breaks when necessary. Better concentration is one of the side effects of mental training.

Observation and attention

She tilts her head a little to the right, gives me a mischievous look. "I'm Susie." To remember the name Susie and everybody else you meet, you have to pay attention when they introduce themselves. Observation and attention can be improved through practice.

Being observant is critical for remembering. To train your ability to observe, study a face. Look at the eyes, the hair and the wrinkles on the forehead. Close your eyes. Try to see the details in face as well as you can. Open your eyes and compare. Add details you missed the first time. Look at teeth, neck and skin. Look at the shadows. Continue observing and recalling until you have a perfect image in you mind. You can do the same exercise with paintings and buildings. Soon your ability to observe will be faster and more precise. A nice way to use observation is to save a perfect picture in your memory. In the autumn of 2004 I became an uncle for the first time. She was christened on New Year's Day 2005. She was sleeping on a rug by the Christmas tree while we where waiting to go to Church. I decided to save that moment forever. Carefully I sat down in the chair next to the tree. Then I studied the clothes she was wearing. Her little tummy moving up and down under the maroon dress. Her breathing is too quiet to hear. The only sounds come from the kitchen and the fireplace. The embroidery on the collar. The knitted blanket she's almost kicked off. The lights from the Christmas tree shining on her peaceful face. I can still see it perfectly clear. Her plum cheeks and the mouth twitching occasionally. A touch of blue on her eyelids. Her arms straight out; the left a little closer to her head than the right. Rolling fingers now and then. The shadows over her face. Growing eyebrows and still an almost bald head. I will never forget this image.

Creating journeys

If you are planning to compete in memory championships, or just memorise for exams, you will need several journeys. To keep control of my journeys I write them down. Having memorised a deck of cards or some other memory event, I re-use the same journeys after a few days. As you read in the chapter on Journeys, there is no reason not to re-use a journey to memorise general knowledge. For exams I use both new and old journeys, but I let the journeys rest until after all the exams are finished before re-using them. There are two effective ways to create journeys. Either you can physically walk through a new journey or you can think about places you have been and roads you have walked.

Mental journeys

The journeys you created at the start of the book were mental journeys; you thought about places you have been. When you think about it you realise that you have already walked through thousands of journeys. It is unlikely you will forget the road you walked to primary school, or the steep hill that seemed never ending. So many things happened on the way to and from school that it is etched into you memory for the rest of your life. Short journeys are easier to handle than long journeys of fifty to a hundred points.

Try to create a journey of ten to twenty points along the road to your old school. Imagine you are in year 3 at school. The backpack is uncomfortable. The books too heavy. What is the first thing you see as you walk out the door? Do you walk down some stairs? Do you walk past some statues? A fire hydrant? Do you pass any scary houses or animals? Are there horses close to the road? Do you see a fountain? Can you hear the sound of the river? Think about your life: where you have lived, gone to school and worked, and create journeys. Houses generally work the best, as the rooms are natural dividers between the points. Shopping malls, houses and public buildings can be the locations getting you top marks at university. The possibilities are endless.

Physical journeys

I find mental journeys to be most effective, but if you run out you can create new journeys physically. You can walk, jog, bicycle, drive, paddle, or whatever else takes your fancy. Follow me on a journey through my hometown to learn how I create a new journey:

I am standing right by the soccer stadium. In front of me the flags on the kiosk are waiving in the wind. The kiosk is my first point. I walk around the corner and see a garage; my second point. I walk past the third point: the stairs. The sun is reflected in the seats in the dugout; the fourth point. Past this is a large wall to kick balls against; point number five. Point six is the large pine tree that I used to pee behind during track & field practice. The mat used for high jump is a perfect point seven. The wind makes the soccer goal squeak; point eight. The shot put area is point nine and, finally I get to point ten, the finish line for the 100-metre sprint.

To make sure that I have the correct order I often walk through the journey a second time. The journey naturally becomes a part of my long-term memory; ready to be used for memorising.

Summary

You have noticed that by using Memo you can, by reading it just once, remember large amounts of information. And the information stays for much longer than usual. The more you have to remember, the more repetitions are necessary – even when using Memo. Memo, however, saves you a lot of time compared with conventional learning and the information you remember is more precise. Less time spent on remembering more.

Focus is often a result of what you have done prior to having to concentrate. To become more focused or to stay focused, it is smart to keep the speed up so that other thoughts cannot interrupt. One of the key things for perfect recall is the quality of the journeys you create. Most journeys can feel a little challenging in the beginning, but you can solve this by writing them down. Once you have used them, or walked through them in your mind a few times, you have enough storage space to memorise hundreds of words in fifteen minutes. With perfect recall.

Memo for general knowledge and in school

Learning is often about remembering. School children and students all over the world are required to remember copious amounts of information, yet very few are given the tools to do this well - they are not taught how to remember. This chapter will provide you with the specific memory tools you need to help you memorise subjects like history, anatomy, languages and many more. Tips for a successful exam will follow at the end of the chapter.

Speed-reading

Do you want to read faster? No need to buy a book on speed-reading. The methods can be summarised in a few paragraphs. Look up from the text and let your eyes glide across the room – from left to right in a slow, steady motion. Do it now. The task is difficult because the eyes want to stop and focus on details. Try the same task again: this time with a finger or pencil as a guide right underneath what you are looking at. Hold the pen 30-40 cms away from your face. What happened? You looked around in one steady eye movement. Yet you still picked up the details in the room.

This method can be easily transferred to reading. You will immediately read faster, as you won't stop or look back. There are two main methods for speed-reading. The most common method is to hold your finger or a pen under the word you want to read, or you could let the pen cover the line you're about to read - hold it horizontally and uncover the line as your read.

Your aim should be to read fast enough to keep other thoughts out of your mind. If you read too slowly, daydreams will compete for you attention and you'll lose focus. The faster you read, more you will have to concentrate to keep up. This will keep other thoughts away and help you remember more. If your attitude is "I've got to read through it one more time anyway," you have already lost – why focus when you will repeat it later? Tell yourself that you only have one chance; that will improve your concentration. Experiment a little and find a quick rhythm you're comfortable with. There may be occasions where a quick scan, followed by a more in-depth study of the material could be smart. If you want to look up words or concepts, mark them with a pencil and come back to them later. The moral of the story: keep a good rhythm and don't stop.

Try to read so fast that you are only able to absorb about half the text. This makes reading easier when you later slow down a little. The speed of your reading will obviously depend on the text and the pleasure you want to get out of it. Kjetill Gunnarson, Norwegian speed-reader, has managed 3050 words per minute in competition. That is 50 words per second! Essentially, competitors scan the text rather than read it. To assess if they actually absorb any of the non-fiction text, they are asked multiple-choice questions about the content. When Kjetill reads fiction, he slows down significantly, as he wants to enjoy the story. Kjetill also subscribes to a lot of different magazines and newspapers: every second week he sits down to read the half metre stack. To start off, he does not read it all, but rather scans them quickly while asking the question: "Is this interesting?" Interesting articles he will rip out and put aside; in the end he may have a stack of articles no more than 5 centimetres high.

Asking himself the question "is this *really* interesting?" he will scan through the articles again and only keep those that really are. He started with half a metre; now he only has a handful left. And only now will he speed-read – even if he is one of the world's best speed-readers.

Reading is like a car trip. You can enjoy the scenery in three different ways. Drive slowly; catch a lot of glimpses but you'll have to constantly check the road ahead. Or you could drive fast but stop occasionally to enjoy the view; you will miss a lot and get to you destination in the same time. The best solution is to have a driver and instead be a passenger and enjoy the scenery the whole time. Think about the pen or finger as your personal driver. It helps you keep the rhythm, and improves your focus.

History and dates

Memo is perfect for anyone with an interest in history. My history Professor kept telling this story about a historian. The historian was asked what is most important in understanding historic events. "Years and dates," he answered. "You have to know what is the cause and what is the effect. You need a chronological understanding of history". There is less focus on remembering historical dates today than there used to be in the past. The focus is supposedly on understanding. Yet you will not understand history if you cannot remember that the Middle Ages came before the Renaissance.

Let's look at how you can easily learn and remember historical dates. Here are three methods for memorising, depending on the time-period of the event and how many dates you want to memorise. Let us have a look at them:

Same Century

Let's say that you want to memorise events from the 20th century.

The advantage of memorising events in the same century is that we can reduce the information we need to remember. To make it even more efficient, we create separate storage areas for each decade of the century. This method is based on dividing your house or school into ten areas. You may end up with something like this:

1900–1909 = Foyer	1950–1959 = Reception
1910–1919 = Classroom	1960–1969 = Notice board
1920–1929 = Library	1970–1979 = Lunchroom
1930–1939 = Computer room	1980–1989 = Oval
1940–1949 = Toilets	1990–1999 = Car park

It is easier to remember which year each area represents if they follow in a sequence, so that the 1930s come after the 1920s. These rooms are your storage area for the events for these time periods. In 1903, the Wright Brothers were the first to actually fly an aeroplane. We will put this event in the foyer, as this represents the first decade of the 1900s. No need to remember the first three digits, which leaves us with 3.

Visualise Orville Wright in the foyer – handcuffed to a plane. The handcuffs remind us of the year. The room (foyer) tells us the first three digits are 190 and we simply add the 3. Hence, the first flight was in 1903.

In 1929 the US stock market crashed, beginning the slide into the Great Depression. Skip the first three digits and we're left with 9. Nine looks like a balloon or an axe. Imagine a big balloon bursting in the library.

We can memorise several events in each area. The 1910s was an eventful decade - World War I and the Russian Revolution, to name a few. In 1914 the Panama Canal was finally completed. We have already memorised associations for the war and the revolution in the classroom, but we can easily add more events. As you have noticed, we use one figure for the year plus one or more as the association for the actual event. For the Panama Canal we'll visualise a panda (Panama) aboard a boat (the association for the number 4) in the classroom.

Think of some locations for events of the 1800s. Memorise that Napoleon lost the Battle of Waterloo in 1815. First you think about your location for 1810 to 1819. Then create an image for the event along with the association for 5. Imagine a scene where the figure for the number five is involved in the battle. The scene is played out in the location you decided on for the 1810s. Imagine the scene once more to reinforce the image you created. First, write down associations for event and figure for the last digit – then try to memorise a few more:

1837 – Morse first exhibits the telegraph

1851 – Gold is discovered in Australia

1871 – Germany is unified as an empire

1884 to 1885 – The Conference of Western powers divides Africa

1889 – The Eiffel tower is built

Same Millennium

To memorise events from an entire millennium we can use a similar method. We create memory storage areas in the same way, but let each area represent a century:

1000–1099 = Hallway	1400–1499 = Bathroom
1100–1199 = Laundry	1500–1599 = Lounge
1200–1299 = Study	1600–1699 = Balcony
1300–1399 = Kitchen	…and so on.

This time we only skip the first two digits, as they represent the room we're storing the year in. You want to remember that Spain conquered Portugal in 1580. Create some associations for Spain and Portugal. A spa could be your association for Spain. Let a glass of port symbolise Portugal. To remember the event I see Mao in my mind - he symbolises the number 80 in the Alternative Double System. Mao pouring water from the spa into the port bottle. Mao's strange behaviour reminds you that Spain (spa) conquered (filling the bottle) Portugal (bottle of port) in 1580. 15 because it happens in the lounge and 80 because Mao is the association for this number. You probably want to remember when Portugal regained independence too. A robot empties the port bottle of spa water on the balcony. The balcony is the 1600s and the robot the association for 40. Hence, the year is 1640. The rest of the picture is enough to remember than Portugal regained independence in 1640.

There is plenty of room in each area. It's almost nostalgic to return to a spot to memorise new knowledge. The first enduring English settlement in the New World began at Jamestown, Virginia in 1607. We walk out to the balcony to join the robot. But now we also see Osama bin Laden (association for 07) eating jam (association for Jamestown) out there. So Jamestown was settled in 1607.

You can also store events that last for several years. The Black Plague wreaked havoc in Europe from 1347 to 1352. I imagine Rod Laver (47) in the kitchen. He stabs (the action for the number 52) a black creature. The creature wears a black robe and carries a scythe. In the olden days people believed that the Grim Reaper brought the plague. I use the same association to remind me of when the Black Plague killed millions in Europe.

Leonardo da Vinci lived from 1452 to 1519. How should we memorise events stretching over centuries? Let's imagine a starfish (52) ignite (action 19) Leonardo da Vinci in the bathroom. We use person 52 to remember da Vinci's year of birth and the action 19 to remember the year of his death. With the action happening in the bathroom we know he was born in the 1400s. That he died in the 1500s is so logical that we don't need to memorise it.

You can upgrade the history methods by adding rooms at the beginning and end of the journey to memorise additional centuries. Ideally the rooms should follow in some sort of linear order.

Longer time periods or only a few dates

1893 - New Zealand gives women the vote.

860 - Vikings in two hundred ships raid Constantinople.

About 1455 - Gutenberg uses movable type to print the Bible, beginning a new era of scholarship and communication.

If you only have ten to twenty years to remember, you can use a different method. You can use the Triple System to translate the year. To memorise Gutenberg - remove the digit for the millennium, as you will remember that anyway, and we are left with 455. In the Triple System 455 is Rus. Choose a keyword, like "print", for the event and add it to the code for the year. Visualise a rusty printing press, or a Russian printing a book. In the year 860, Vikings, in two hundred ships, raided Constantinople. Here we have the three digits already, but our natural memory will still remember that this happened before the year 1000. Imagine a Viking playing with a mafia boss (8 is m, 6 is 'a' sound as in hay and 0 is f). This is fun; let's do a few more!

In 1893 women in New Zealand were allowed to vote. Remove the first digit and we are left with 893 – which becomes mob. O as in low. We add a y and get Moby. Women celebrated by using Moby Dick's blowhole as the ballot box.

If you want to add the years to your long-term memory, you should memorise them in rooms or along a journey. If not, you risk that the images will just float around in your mind and will be hard to retrieve when you need them. If all you need to remember is the three events above, you will only need three rooms or points – just let each scene play out in each room.

Summary

By now you will be able to remember years and historical dates better than most people – unless they use Memo too. The best part is that you effectively let your sense of place represent time – i.e. you place a symbol for the year in a tangible room that represents time. How to memorise historical events:

- Choose one or more keywords for the event
- Reduce the number of digits for the year
- Translate the number into an association
- Visualise the keyword for the event along with the association for the number
- Save the image in an area or a journey by visualising

Languages

Learning a language is mostly about memorising words. The French word for yellow is *jaune*; it rhymes with Sean Connery's first name. Associations like this one can make it easier to learn a new vocabulary.

But associations have a tendency to just float around in your mind if you create a lot of them. This is why locations are so important if you want to effectively learn a new language. Think about a town or a suburb you know really well - this will become your mental dictionary. Here you can store foreign words in your long-term memory. You will save the words in an orderly system; that way you can easily retrieve them when you need to. The reason we use a town we know well to store the new vocabulary is that the place is already part of the long-term memory.

In school we had to rote learn new words. Generally they were stored in our short-term memory. Through drawn-out and painful repetition, the new words slowly became automatic. Yet, after a few years without practicing your hard-earned language skills, half your vocabulary disappeared. The method you will learn here will put the new words straight into your long-term memory. The words become part of your town.

Germanic languages have three genders for the substantives: masculine, feminine and neuters. Italian, Spanish, Portuguese, French and Arabic have two genders: masculine and feminine. Let us use Italian in this example. I have choosen to store my Italian words in my hometown. A river runs through the town, dividing it in half. Hence, the river works as a perfect barrier between the masculine and feminine substantives. On the north side I will store the masculine words, while the feminine words are stored on the south side.

The articles *il* and *la* tell us the gender of the substantive. Hence, to be able to express ourselves, we must remember both the meaning of the word, as well as the word's gender. *La borsa* means handbag. This is, as we can see, a feminine word. We ignore the article, *la* and focus only on the word. *Borsa*, I associate with Boris (Yeltsin). The association is ready and we can save the word in our long-term memory. As we know, the feminine words are memorised on the south side of the river. Try to find a logical location for storing the word – this makes it easier to retrieve when you need it. So why not a store selling handbags? Imagine Boris sticking out of one of the handbags. When we need to look-up the word in the mental dictionary, we just walk into the handbag store. As it is located on the south side, we know that the word is feminine. Boris in the handbag gives us the word. Hence, handbag is *la borsa* in Italian. Now you know that. Maybe you will never have to look it up again. And you haven't even revised yet. It is almost too easy.

Il regalo means gift. As before, we drop the article – *il* and create an association for *regalo*. This word can be quite hard to find an association for, but you could imagine the Queen's royal outfits – her regalia: jewellery and crown. Remember, the association does not have to be perfect. The word is stored in the gift shop on the north side of the river. Imagine the Queen giving away her outfits to the customers. We have now added another word to our mental dictionary – a dictionary with infinite storage space. Italian is a logical language. Masculine words end with *–o*. Feminine words end with an *–a* - although there are some exceptions to these rules. The word *fiore* (flower) is masculine, even if it ends with *–e*. Words that end with *–e* in Italian can be either masculine or feminine. Good thing we don't have to worry about that, as we know *fiore* is masculine based on its location in the flower shop on the north side of the river. Not all substantives ending with an *–o* are masculine and certain words that end with *–a* don't conform to the rule for feminine words. We know from life experience that there are no rules without exceptions, yet in the mental dictionary there are no exceptions. Every word on the south side is feminine. All the words on the north side are masculine. No exceptions whatsoever.

Similar words can be memorised by visualising a flag as a symbol to show that the words are pronounced the same way. As we can see, visualisation is a good method to make it easier to remember information. Combined with location, we can remember enormous amount of knowledge. Quite often we learn groups of words at the same time: colours, numbers or body parts. Groups like these can be saved in separate spaces. I have memorised the French words for colours in a barn:

- Red in French is *rouge* – which reminds me of make-up. I find a natural place in the barn for red – the outside wall is bright red. I visualise a girl putting rouge (make-up) on the wall.

- *Vert* is green. It is pronounced without saying the t. The bales of hay are green, so I store the colour where the hay is stored. I imagine the bales of hay as the foundation for a veranda.

- Yellow is *jaune* – which rhymes with Sean. Sean Connery is playing with the yellow machine in the barn.

- Light blue is *bleu clair* in French. My friend Clare comes running out of the barn, choking on something she's eaten - her face turning light blue – blue Clare.

- Dark blue is *bleu foncé*. There is a fence around the barn. Make it dark blue.

When you are looking for a colour, you know where to look it up. All the colours are in and around the barn, in logical places. You learn the words quickly and avoid mixing them. You don't have to think of Sean Connery every time you are looking for the French word for yellow. The method is your safety net until your new vocabulary becomes automatic. Obviously you will have to do more revision the more words you are trying to learn. But with this method you don't have to revise over and over twenty times like you would if you were learning the traditional way.

To learn the names of body parts we use the body (naturally) as the location. Here are four words. Imagine a male body, as the words are masculine.

- The thumb is *le pouce* in French. Rhymes with "puss". Store the word on your own thumb (if you're a man). If the word was feminine, I would have stored it on a female. No need to know the article, le, as I imagine a cat sitting on my thumb.

- *Le bras* is the arm - pronounced "bra". Visualise a bra around your arm.
- The wrist is *le poignet*. My association is a pony. It works, even if the sounds don't match perfectly. Imagine a pony on your wrist. A cute little miniature pony.
- *Le cou* is the neck. Pronounced "koo". I imagine a cuckoo clock around my neck – someone got angry with me and banged it over my head. It is important to visualise the association you have decided on.

All these words were masculine. There is no doubt that cat is masculine, as it is on my male thumb.

- *La joue* is the chin. My location for feminine words is a female friend. Visualise a shoe print on the girls chin, as shoe sounds a lot like joue.
- *La jambe* is the leg, and sounds like sham(poo). Imagine shampoo running down her leg.
- *La cheville* is French for ankle. Visualise the girl with a tattoo of a Chevy (car) on her ankle.
- *La bouche* is the mouth – rhymes with "bosh". Imagine George W Bush in the girl's mouth.

Associating *la jambe* with shampoo may seem like a stretch, but your brain can do this instantly. Never underestimate your own brainpower. Use associations that feel natural. It is important that you visualise the association properly the first time. If you do that, you may only have to revise once, although a few more repetitions won't hurt. It could be tempting to store *la cheville* (the ankle) on a Chevy – e.g. a Chevy driving over an ankle. But you then lose the advantage of storing the word based on gender – something that is very important in many languages. In addition, you will struggle to find the word when you need it. Should you need the word ankle in a conversation, you won't know where to look - it could be anywhere. There is no logic in searching around a Chevy car. So save the Chevy on the girl's ankle instead.

You can learn numbers by using the Single System. The association for 4 is a sailboat, a swan for 2, etc. Think about the association for 1, a flagpole. Imagine someone playing the card game Uno on the flagpole. *Uno* is the number 1 in Italian. Imagine a swan sitting on a doe (female deer). *Due* is 2 in Italian, but the word is pronounced 'doe' and we want to store the pronunciation. 3 is *tre* in Italian – handcuff a tree. *Quattro* is 4. Imagine an Audi Quattro (all-wheel drive) crashing into a sailboat.

Dividing the town into sections, like the north and south side of the river, is perfect for learning substantives. What about verbs, adjectives, pronouns and all the other things you can never quite remember? Choose a few natural locations. You will need quite a lot of space to store a lot of verbs, maybe even a few different locations. The verbs you can store at the fancy gym with a swimming pool and those tennis courts outside. A park, your school or the nearby museum is perfect for adjectives. Store the pronouns in the post office. Do not worry if the gym is in the masculine (north) side of town. Only verbs have access to the gym anyway. To laugh is *ridere* in Italian. Visualise the lady at reception laughing at the horse riders trotting into the gym. *Rompere* in Italian means to crush. Visualise the body builders at the gym romping through the building with dumbbells. A brutally effective way to remember. Italian is special when it comes to verbs: almost all end in –are or -ere, a few end with -ire and even less end in -si. The ending of the verb decides the plural forms. Personally, I have saved all the verbs ending in -are in one part of the gym and -ere in a different part. Verbs ending in

-ire I've moved to a different building. Maybe you want to store one type of Italian verbs at your primary school, another type at work and the third type at the oval.

By storing them in separate locations, you can remove the last three letters of the word. To run is correre. I store –ere verbs in one part of the gym. Hence, the last three letters can be dropped, correre, and we can imagine a stream of cordial running through the gym and down to the tennis court. In the dressing room, a girl is reading a leg. This reminds me that to read is leggere in Italian. In addition I know the inflection of the verb; it happens in the –ere part of the building. The amount of information is reduced to the minimum.

If you for whatever reason have to learn a lot of words starting with fa, you can store them all in the same location. The place reminds you of the fa-; therefore you have reduced the information you have to remember. Conjunctions are indeclinable words which serve to join together sentences, words, phrases, etc. A good place to store them would be the bridge across the river – the bridge that joins the feminine part to the masculine part of town. The word we want to memorise is for - or *per* in Italian. Imagine a Ford on the bridge. Who's driving? Your Swedish friend Per of course. The word and can be written & - it looks like a snowman. Instead of pebbles for eyes, the snowman has the sign for the Euro, €, as his eyes. Now you will remember that and is *e* in Italian.

Both *ma* and *peró* means but. Visualise your mum (ma) handing out pears (peró) and butter on the bridge. The memory method is great for grammar too. Anomalous verbs can also be easily memorised in a journey.

Summary

The method can be used for any language. The recipe is to think about a place you already know well and then divide it into parts, depending on the number of genders in the language. No need to draw a physical map. If the language has three genders, you make the mental divisions. Rivers, bridges, streets, landmarks, shopping malls and lakes work well as dividers. Place groups of similar words in the same place. Create an association that will remind you of the word. Be consistent in creating associations either based on pronunciation or spelling. Visualise the association along with the meaning of the word in a logical location.

Vocabulary in the neighbourhood

Andi Bell taught me a different method for learning new words. He divides his neighbourhood based on the alphabet. The garden is G, the park is P and the kitchen represents K. This is how he split up the entire neighbourhood into 26 locations. We will memorise the words based on the first letter in the English word. To clap (your hands) is *klatschen* in German. We memorise the word in the courtyard, as all words starting with C are stored here. *Klatschen* sounds a bit like clutch. Imagine a person clapping a pedal (the clutch) in the courtyard.

- A cup is *die Tasse* in German. You have your C-words in the courtyard. Imagine Tasmania (Tassie) in the courtyard. Tasmania is shaped quite like a cup. As you can see, the word is feminine. We place the substantives around the room based on gender. Feminine at the left, neuters in the middle and masculines to the right. The advantage of placing words based on gender is that you will automatically know the gender just by seeing where it is placed.
- The bed is *das Bett*. All B words are stored in the basement. It works quite well to have Batman (bettman) in the basement. In the middle of the basement, as Bett is of neuter gender.

If I am stuck in the middle of a conversation with a German, I just have to look around my neighbourhood and find the words I have stored. I always know where to find the words and if I have saved it, I will find it. Once I have used the word a few times, I will not longer have to look it up. The method is perfect for the holiday, or to expand your vocabulary in a language you learnt in school. You can have a neighbourhood for each language you want to learn. The German may have an Italian friend who is notoriously late. *Aspettare* is Italian for waiting. Memorise the word in the wardrobe, which is where we store all W words for our Italian dictionary. Visualise Peter sitting on his arse, in the wardrobe, waiting.

The other way around

You can also memorise the words based on the first letter of the foreign word. This can be smart when reading foreign languages. If you look up *partire* in your dictionary, you may have forgotten the meaning of the word when you run into it the next week. So you might as well store *partire* in the neighbourhood; your mental dictionary.

- *Girare* means to turn. We store the word in the garage. Visualise the giraffe run out of the garage and turn towards you.
- If you store words to look up while reading, you will not have to store them based on pronounciation. You can save *scrivere*, meaning to write, in the Shed. Imagine a person writing scribbles on the shed - perhaps Italian graffiti.

Geography

In my early teens I spent a week wandering around in the mud at a scout camp. I still have a lot of memories from the camp and every time I hear or read about the place, I associate the news with one of my many memories. Wagga Wagga, on the other hand, I have no interest in hearing about. No reason to ignore Wagga Wagga, but I have no connection to the place. Until I can connect an association to Wagga Wagga, the town will just be another word to me. Preferably, we could travel around the world and acquire associations for every town and country. Fortunately, there are cheaper ways to learn geography. In North America, there are twenty-four countries north of the Panama Canal. First, decide on a journey with twenty-four points. Then create associations for all the countries and their capitals. The associations should be people or items associated with the country, or simply direct associations for the words. Cuba makes me think of Fidel Castro and Canada reminds me of maple leaf. I have no associations for Dominica, but the word is similar to domino. The capital of Dominica tells me nothing, so I think of a rose, as the city is called Roseau.

The first point in my journey is the flowerbed. This is where I place the northernmost country, Canada – maple leaf being the obvious association. I think of an otter for the capital, Ottawa. Hence, I visualise an otter eating maple leafs in the flowerbed. The second point is the barbecue. I imagine George W Bush washing his clothes in diesel. Bush is my association for the US and him washing clothes in diesel reminds me that the capital is Washington, D.C.

By the big rock, which is my third point, I see a NASA astronaut in pyjamas. A pyjama is my image for the Bahamas; NASA is the association for the capital, Nassau. Several countries have capitals that share their name with the country. In these cases the association for the capital is simply a white flag. When I get to Panama, I visualise a panda (association for Panama) waving a white flag – the capital is Panama City. If you like to, you can make your journey into a circle around a building or around your house. This way the associations for the countries and their capitals are placed in a circle. A similar circle can be drawn on the map, from Canada and the US in the north, via the small Caribbean islands and back up through Latin America. This way we kill two birds with one stone. First of all, we memorise the countries and capitals in a journey. Secondly, the journey will tell us where the countries are on the map (this is also true if the journey is linear). Bahamas is the point before Cuba. Thus, Bahamas is north of Cuba. After Cuba we create an image for Haiti and its capital, Port-au-Prince. We will then know that Haiti is south of Cuba. Lastly, we get to Jamaica. The journey tells us that Jamaica is right in the middle of the Caribbean. The best part of the method is that we learn cold, hard facts while learning the geographic location at the same time.

Here is a list over countries, capitals and suggestions for associations for the first six:

Country	Association	Capital	Association
Canada	Maple leaf	Ottawa	Otter
USA	George Bush	Washington	Washing in diesel
Bahamas	Pyjamas	Nassau	NASA astronaut
Cuba	Fidel Castro	Havana	Cigar
Haiti	Hair	Port-au-Prince	Prince
The Dominican Republic	Domino	Santo Domingo	Dingo
Puerto Rico		San Juan	
Antigua and Barbuda		St. John's	
St. Kitts and Nevis		Basseterre	
Dominica		Roseau	
St. Lucia		Castries	
Barbados		Bridgetown	
St. Vincent and Grenadines		Kingstown	
Grenada		St. George's	
Trinidad and Tobago		Port of Spain	
Panama		Panama City	
Costa Rica		San José	
Nicaragua		Managua	
Honduras		Tegucigalpa	
El Salvador		San Salvador	
Guatemala		Guatemala City	
Belize		Belmopan	
Mexico		Mexico City	
Jamaica		Kingston	

Make associations and try to memorise the list. To remember the list for the rest of your life, you will probably have to revise a few times. But it is quick and easy when you use journeys and have the associations written down.

Maps as journeys

Maps almost work as journeys or locations by themselves. You have a fair idea of the shape of South America. You can place the associations straight on the map instead of creating a journey around the house. Maybe all you want to learn is the names of the countries. Imagine Pelé (association for Brazil) running up the east coast of South America, doing a fancy move on a French guy – probably Zinedine Zidane (French Guyana). Pelé is in fine form and does a tunnel on a surfer (Surinam), gets tackled by a gnu (Guyana) and so on.

In Africa, on the western side from the equator and south, we find Gabon, (Democratic) Republic of Congo, Angola and Namibia. Using the first letter, we get GRAN. To remember the countries you can visualise your Grandma on the map. Turkey, Iran, Pakistan and India form a long belt of landmass. Imagine some Native-Americans ("Indians") trying to erect a tipi. Finally they've made it to where they initially got their name. Countries in central and eastern Europe can be hard to stay on top of. Visualise SAUR – sour cream – over the top of the countries Slovenia, Austria, Hungary and Romania.

It actually reminds me a little of a rhyme a friend learned in school. The seven continents (Europe, Antarctica, Asia, Africa, North America, South America) can be remembered as follows: "Eat An Aspirin After A Nighttime Snack"

Associations

If you want to memorise the names and capitals of all the countries in the world, you may struggle to come up with associations for all of them. Often it can be helpful to have a set association for countries with similar endings. Several countries in Asia end with –stan. The set association for –stan can really be anything. Like a broom. In the chapter on journeys, you learnt how to create associations based on word plays, celebrities or something else we associate with the country we wish to remember.

Anatomy

The body has been used as a location for knowledge throughout history. You may know how to use the knuckles on your hand to work out how many days there are in a month. Make a fist of your hand, with the knuckles up. Start with January at the index finger knuckle. Every knuckle represents a month with 31 days and in between the knuckles represents a month with 30 days (except February of course). When you get to July (31 days), you will have run out of knuckles, so just start again at the index finger knuckle – August has 31 days.

A nice way to learn the nine times table is to use your fingers. Hold your hands up with your palms facing you. To get the answer to one times nine, you bend one thumb. Count the number of fingers to get the answer. Bend another finger, so that two are bent. Count the remaining fingers, and you have the answer to two times nine. Eight fingers left; the answer is eighteen. Bend three fingers. Seven fingers still straight – nine times three is twenty-seven. This way you can easily learn the nine times table all the way to ninety.

In both examples we use a classic method for learning. We connect old knowledge (the sequence of the months) to known surroundings (the knuckles), while learning something new (the number of days in each month). The body can be used as a location in many ways. Physio and medical students imagine a lot of weird things happening on the body to learn anatomy. To learn the most important part of the brain I use my hand. A fist, seen from the side, looks like the brain in profile. Visualise images to remember the different parts of the brain.

Anatomy based on a journey

The body is essentially a journey already – a good place to use as location for the names of our muscles. We could imagine a gymnast performing on a trapeze on our shoulder, as the muscle is called trapezius. But as we have lot of muscles, we would end up with a confusing number of gymnasts, fruits, things and celebrities visualised on our body. In the last chapter we learnt how to memorise geography. Muscles, ligaments and bones can be memorised the same way – in a journey like we memorised the countries and capitals in. We also knew where the countries where placed based on their position along the journey.

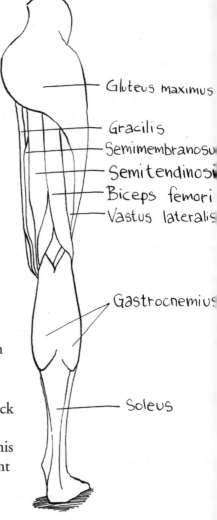

Let us see how the muscles at the back of our body can be memorised – in Latin called the posteriore side. In this example we need a journey with eight points, where we will memorise the most important muscles. Let's start with the leg.

The first muscle is soleus. Create an association, maybe a sun. Visualise the sun having fallen out of the sky at the first point. We not only memorise the name of the muscles, but also their location relative to the other muscles. The sun at the first point helps us remember that the muscle is called soleus. We also know that the muscle is in the lower part of the leg, as it is the first point in our journey. At the next point we memorise the muscle that is directly above, Gastrocnemius. And the journey goes on. Just as we know that point five comes before point six, we will know where the muscles are located. If your Latin is good, feel free to use the meaning of the name of the muscle as your association if this is easier than creating a separate association or word play. The seat muscle is called gluteus maximus. At the last point I visualise Russell Crowe in Gladiator. He played the character Maximus, a large gladiator. Memorising the muscles in the upper body can be more difficult, as the muscles are not conveniently placed in a linear order. But as long as you decide on an order before you memorise the muscles you will have no trouble using a journey for these too.

First Aid

Most of us have been to first aid courses. But do you remember what to do if you arrive at the scene of an accident? It can be a very stressful and chaotic situation – but it is important to remain calm. Knowing what to do can be the difference between life and death. You may already know the acronym DRABC (Danger, Response, Airway, Breathing, Circulation) – if you do and know what to do at each step, that's good. Memorising what to do at each step will help you stay calm and in control. Having secured the area and worked out whom to help first, you should follow these instructions, based on advice from firstaidinternational.com.au. Some of the key words are in bold - we will have a proper look at these later:

Ask for the person's name and gently squeeze their shoulder. **Is the person conscious?** Yes: calm the person, observe and look for injuries. No: **Open mouth** and check for foreign material. If yes, place in recovery position and **remove foreign objects** from airway. Check **breathing** and pulse. Look, hear, feel to see if patient is breathing. Is the injured person breathing? **Yes:** place in

recovery position. Call 000. Observe. Manage injuries. **No**: Call **000** immediately. If alone with the patient, place in recovery position before calling. Turn person onto back, tilt head, and give **two initial breaths**. Ensure chest rises with each breath. Has breathing returned? **Yes**: place in **recovery position**, check regularly for signs of life. **No**: Start **CPR. Use two hands with fingers interlocked. Give 30 compressions, straight down, on lower half of breastbone**. Tilt head, lift chin and give two breaths. Alternate **30 compressions with two breaths** until medical help arrives.

The words in bold are the keywords for first aid. Let us memorise them in a journey. Journeys are perfect for events that need to happen in a certain order. Notice that the key words have been reduced to the bare minimum. The more you need to remember, the harder it is. Here are the key words in a list:

1. Conscious?
2. Open mouth
3. Remove foreign objects
4. Breathing?
5. Yes: recovery position
6. No: 000
7. Two breaths.
8. Two hands with fingers interlocked. Lower breastbone
9. 30 compressions, straight down.
10. Two breaths. 30 compressions.

Create a ten-point journey and memorise this list just like you memorised the elements of the periodic table. If you know the emergency number you just memorise a phone.

You will remember the images for a long time. But something as important as first aid should be revised frequently. Why not revise while your waiting for the bus? The information is already in your mind, so you might as well walk through the journey now and then. You will be surprised how quickly you can do it. If you have you forgotten a point, you can have a quick look at the list above and reinforce the association. This may be the most important first aid course you have ever done. Simply because you will remember what you have learned.

Maths

$$Cos^2x + E^*\delta = \int k / 10 \, dx$$

The hardest formulas are those that seem meaningless. The formula above is made up and totally meaningless. But let's assume that you had to learn an equation like this for an exam. How would you memorise it?

Formulas that you remember anyway – either because you have used them a lot or they are simply easy – you obviously don't have to memorise. When you come across more complex formulas you can use Memo. The trouble is that it can be harder to work out *how* to use Memo for formulas than actually memorising them.

If you find the formula hard to remember because it is too similar to other formulas - then I recommend you only focus on parts of the formula. Lets say that the only difference between the formula above and similar formulas is the *cos* and *k* part.

$$Cos^2x + E^*\delta = \int k / 10 \, dx$$
$$Sin^2x + E^*\delta = \int i / 10 \, dx$$
$$Tan^2x + E^*\delta = \int gt / 10 \, dx$$

In cases like these you only have to memorise the structure of the first formula. Then you memorise the unique features of the rest – in this case *sin - i* and *tan - gt*. The general structure may be so simple that all you need to memorise is the unique parts of all three.

At other times, the formula is alone, with nothing to compare it to. You can still memorise only parts of the formula. "Me Tarzan..." easily reminds us of "You Jane". If one domino falls, the rest should follow. You will know that dx comes after $\int$ if you study maths. No need to memorise that. Remembering $E^*\delta$ and k may be enough remind you of the rest of the formula. Use the domino principle wherever you can. Trust your brain.

Some formulas are simply too hard to remember – and hard to work out how to memorise. If you have to memorise the entire formula you should divide and conquer – divide it into suitable chunks. Make associations first.

$$Cos^2x + E^*\delta = \int k / 10 \, dx$$

Cos may remind you of cosmetics and 2 looks like a swan. That gives you two things to remember. It could be advantageous to create just one association for Cos^2. For example a *costume* (cos two). The advantage is that now we only have one thing to remember, not two. Since none of the formulas have y in place of x, I choose to ignore the x following Cos^2. Memorising addition or multiplication is mostly unnecessary, but more about that later. δ is the sign for Delta. The association for $E^*\delta$ could be *Eddie Murphy – Ed*. Continue until you have made associations for the entire formula.

Creating associations is often the hardest part of memorising. You just have to cut away the fat – decide on an association and move on. If you get bogged down you might lose your motivation.

Journeys are generally best for memorising formulas. When you recall, you will find the costume and Eddie Murphy. You don't even have to study maths to know that it means Cos^2x and $E\delta$, at least if you made the associations yourself. The associations should be enough to tell you that there is a + after Cos^2x and * between E and delta. The same goes for = and /. But if these are hard to remember you just memorise them too.

If you ever wonder how much to memorise, you can think backwards. Is it conceivable that a costume and Eddie Murphy are enough to remember + and *? If yes, then no need to memorise them.

Memorising

$$Cos^2x + E^*\delta = \int k / 10 \, dx$$

Costume and *Eddie Murphy* are the first two associations. Let us say that we memorise everything after = to be safe. The first sign $\int$ is integral, while k is a variable. Create an association like *inseKt*. My association for division is a *knife* and the association for 10 is *Maradona*. That dx is at the end of the formula is logical, as we have an integral so there is no need to memorise it. I write down the associations in a list. Costume, Eddie Murphy, inseKt, knife and Maradona. The formula has been reduced to five visual words that can be memorised in a journey. Or perhaps just one or two words to remember the entire formula.

"Ok, I understand that I probably have to remember the formula, but it is pointless when I don't understand how to use it." Understanding is up to you. Going to class will obviously help. The recipe above is meant to help you remember. Remembering it can help you understand. And if you understand it, then your memory will no longer be your limitation, as you have memorised it.

Simple formulas

You can use one of the numerical systems to remember and make formulas visual. The formula for the area of a triangle is base multiplied by height divided by two, or ½ bh. Imagine a triangle (the musical instrument) used as a knife, chopping a Buddha statue in half.

1 kilo is approximately 2.2 pounds. Using the Double System we get tt, tooth, the symbol for 22. As always, if you have a few formulas to learn, you should memorise the formulas in a location. That means visualising them in a suitable location – the tooth on the kitchen or bathroom scales for example.

In maths you have to remember the correct order of calculations:

1. Brackets
2. Multiplications/divisions
3. Additions/subtractions

Try to create an extended acronym from the initial letters:
B M D A S

Biochemistry and organising knowledge

To illustrate how you can organise and compress the amount of information you need to remember, we will look at a chemical formula. Medical students generally have to know the formula for pyruvate:

The students have to know both the name of the formula and its structure. Most of us are not experts in biochemistry, yet we can spot recurring patterns. The pattern above $C = O$ in pyruvate shows up in many chemical formulas. Create an association for the pattern. I imagine a rabbit. When you come across the pattern in other formulas you just have to bring the rabbit out. C = O is also a common pattern. Create an association – maybe a bicycle. The part of the formula under C = O may remind you of metal, as CH3 is a methyl-group.

To remember the structural formula, you can imagine a rabbit cycling over metal (association for methyl). To secure good recall you should visualise the image in a journey. Yes, creating set associations for patterns will take some extra time, but the advantage is that learning new formulas will be a breeze.

Reducing information

You can also reduce the amount of information to make it easier to memorise. If you wish to remember that the Warsaw Treaty was signed in 1955, you can remove 19 and focus on 55. That it happened in 1955 and not 1855 is so obvious that you will remember that anyway. Group and reduce when you can, and visualise what you need to remember in a journey. Do not spend time and effort on what you already know or can easily remember – focus on the challenging information. A newspaper once wanted tips on a simple method for remembering the Government Ministers and Secretaries. Malcolm Turnbull is the Minister for Water and Environment. If you remember the last name you are likely to remember the first name too. Reduce the amount of information by focusing only on the surname. One tip is to find natural places to store politicians – in or around a house or neighbourhood. Visualise a bull (association for Turnbull) swimming in the pool. Maybe it has turned over and is doing backstroke. If you are trying to remember what the water-guy's name is, ask yourself: where did I store the Water Minister? In the pool, where there is plenty pf water. What do I see? A bull. Turnbull it is. Save the Minister for Agriculture in the garden, the transport Minister on the stairs, and the Minister for foreign affairs outside the neighbour's door. Group and reduce when you can and use a location when visualising what you want to remember.

Speed-studying: How to pass exams in two days

My parents never saw my marks from high school. Later I learnt memory techniques. As you read in the introduction, I did very well in my "extinct religions" exam, having studied for only two days and with no prior knowledge or lecture attendance. Since then I have passed several written exams the same way. I have gone from an average of 3.81 (out of 6) in high school - well below the average student – to a credit in Women's and Gender studies on seven hours of memorising. Two lectures and three days of memorising resulted in a distinction in Social Anthropology. Written exams in Norway go for six hours, asking you to explain, analyse, elaborate and compare complex questions drawn from the entire syllabus. You simply cannot BS your way through. Several friends have used Memo with great results in Psychology. Thousands of people that have bought the book have done really well in anything from astrology to psychology and law. How do we do it? Obviously, everybody should go to lectures and read the material long before the exam. However, if you choose to do the exam after seven hours, or a week, of studying, with no prior knowledge, there are several important steps to keep in mind. First of all, reduce the syllabus. The entire syllabus can be several thousand pages of reading, but no one can remember it all. Even the professor will say there is no point in remembering it all. Generally, you only need to know a small part of the syllabus to pass the exam. You don't have the time to read it all anyway. The best way to reduce the amount of material is to copy lecture notes or summaries. Lecture notes are generally a very good indicator of what is important for the exam. The next step is to eliminate unnecessary information. Write down keywords while you read. Some keywords are hard to visualise, so you will have to create associations for them. After all this, memorise the associations in a journey or at another suitable location. Keywords are designed to help you remember all the additional knowledge you have acquired in the subject.

Memorising

Many textbooks have already highlighted keywords - psychology textbooks being a prime example.

In psychology, students are expected to understand a lot of concepts and definitions. Here is an example, from a psychology book, of two different methods of persuasion:

> "The powerful **norm of reciprocity** involves the expectation that when others treat us well, we should respond in kind.
>
> In the 1970s, members of the Hare Krishna Society approached passers-bys and gave them a small flower. If a passer-by refused, the member said *"Please. It is a gift for you."* Reluctantly, people often accepted. Then the member asked for a donation. People felt pressure to reciprocate, donated money and often threw the flower away.
>
> Thus to get you to comply with a request, I can do something nice for you now – such as an unsolicited favour – in hope that you will feel pressure to reciprocate later when I present you my request.
>
> Now consider the **door-in-the-face-technique**: A persuader makes a large request, expecting you to reject it (you slam the door in the persuader's face) and then presents a smaller request. Telemarketers feast on this technique. Rather than ask you directly for a modest monetary contribution to some organisation or cause, they first ask for a much larger contribution, knowing that you will say no. After you politely refuse, they ask for the smaller contribution. In one experiment, after people declined an initial request to donate $25 to a charity, they were more likely to donate $2. To be effective, the same persuader must make both requests. The persuader 'compromises' by making a second, smaller request, so we feel pressure

to reciprocate by complying. Refusing the first request also may produce guilt, and complying with the smaller request may help us reduce guilt or feel socially responsible."

(Passer and Smith, 2004, page 607)

The authors have highlighted *norm of reciprocity* and *door-in-your-face method*. It is important to be able to explain these concepts; it will be smart to memorise keywords relating to them. Our first step was to read the text to gain an understanding that will let us elaborate on the keywords. To remember the keywords, we need somewhere to save them – journeys being the obvious example. Keywords for these two concepts can be memorised in a park, along with other keywords from the psychology syllabus. In my journey, I have stopped by a large tree trunk in the park. I imagine a priest handing out a rose. By the next point, which is the bench, I see a salesman with his face smashed up by a door. Continue memorising keywords like these. Afterwards you should repeat the images. Some concepts can seem really hard to memorise, but even the paragraph below is possible.

"German physiologist Ernst Weber discovered in the 1830s that there is some degree of lawfulness in the range of sensitivities within our sensory systems. **Weber's law** states that the difference threshold, or jnd, is directly proportional to the magnitude of the stimulus with which the comparison is being made and can be expressed as a Weber fraction. For example, the jnd value for weights is a Weber fraction of approximately 1/50. This means that if you lift a weight of 50 grams, a comparison weight must be at least 51 grams in order for you to be able to judge it as heavier. If the weight were 500 grams, a second weight must be at least 510 grams (i.e., 10/500 g) for you to discriminate between them."

(Passer and Smith, 2004, page 113)

Keywords

Which keywords and how many keywords you use depend entirely on the subject in question. The most important part is the type of words we create, as these are the words we will visualise and later recall to remember the rest of the knowledge we possess. From the paragraph on Weber's Law we might choose to focus on two keywords: *Weber* and *weight*. Weber reminds us of his law, who discovered (or created) it and what it is about. Weight reminds us of how the law works in practice. These are the two keywords to memorise in the journey. I would imagine a kitchen scale trapped in a spider web, as spider web works well as an association for Weber. The paragraph on Weber's Law is complicated, but imagine having to remember it for exam without using Memo. In the chapter on Myths you can read more about memorising vs. understanding.

You should write down the keywords and associations as a list, like those you memorised in the chapter on Journeys. By doing that you can memorise a lot quicker and revision is easier. Try to memorise using a fairly quick rhythm. Don't add too many details to the image. Some journalists ask if this simply reduces knowledge to something as trivial as laundry lists. Rather, it reduces what you have to remember anyway to laundry lists. Instead of mindless rote learning, you save time by memorising and thereby saving the knowledge in your long-term memory.

Revision

Having memorised keywords, you should always repeat the images. If your journey consists of several hundred keywords several revisions may be necessary, but you will revise quicker and quicker each time. There are several different ways to revise. One way is to re-read the keywords and then re-imagine your associations; maybe adding some more detail. Another revision method is to test if you actually remember the images. The last method really isn't necessary

– but if you have plenty of time and want to test yourself before the exam. If you have some time to spare you can read through your notes and summaries; this improves your ability to elaborate on the keywords. If you are using a lot of different journeys for your keywords, you should memorise which journeys you have used to speed up your recall.

Even in the exam hall you can add to your knowledge while waiting for the exam to start. For this to be a useful method you should memorise the keywords as you read the new material.

Initial-letter-words and compression

While memorising the syllabus you can compress, reduce and group information, just like you read in the chapter on biochemistry. To remember the order of the Greek philosophers Socrates, Plato and Aristotle you can create the initial-letter-word SPA. Hence, you can visualise the image in one point instead of three – saving points in your journey while only having to remember one image.

You can learn more about initial-letter-words in the chapter called *Other Memory Methods*. Sometimes we can compress lists of info into one image. Psychological research shows that people in need are most likely to receive help from others based on three factors:

- Similarity. If behaviour, nationality or other characteristics are similar, the chance of receiving help increases.
- Gender. Men prefer to help women in need rather than men in need. Women don't discriminate.
- Justice. The likelihood of receiving help increases if people think the person in need is not responsible for his/her predicament. (Passer and Smith, 2004, page 624)

A list like this you can compress into three keywords: similarity, gender, and justice. Make three associations and visualise at one point in a journey. Imagine a man and a woman (gender), a club (association for justice) a sim-card (similarity). The keywords will help us remember what we know about the topic.

Recall

There is no need to write down all your keywords once the exam starts. The keywords are saved in the long-term memory and they are not going away anytime soon. Take your time to read through the questions, enjoy some chocolate. When you have decided on a plan of action, you pick the appropriate journeys. Then you wander through your journeys – writing down what you see and experience. By now you should have an impressive list of keywords to base your answers on!

If the question relates to social thinking and behaviour I look in the park, where I know the knowledge is saved. I write down the associations I see in the park and eventually I get to the tree trunk. This is where I come across the priest with the rose and later, by the bench I see the door-in-your-face salesman. Rather than spending your time trying to wrestle the knowledge from the memory, you can create a much more in-depth analysis of the topic. You know that you have recalled the most important keywords and that you can elaborate on each of them. The priest reminds you of Hare Krishna, of the reciprocity of good deeds, and pressure (the norm of reciprocity). The poor salesman reminds you of large and small requests, the experiment with $25 and $2, the feeling of guilt (the door-in-your-face method).

Quite often the keywords turn into a natural outline for writing your answers. Sometimes you will forget the odd association. Don't panic, just move on to the next point and write down what you see. The forgotten keyword will usually show up again. If you have memorised properly you should expect a recall rate of at least 95% -

of course depending on how much time you spent memorising and how many times you revised. Still, 95% recall on a few hundred keywords should give you a pretty good mark.

Preparation

Before you try to pass an exam on only a week or a day of study you will have to prepare. You need a lot of available storage space. That means that you will have to create or decide on journeys before you start memorising. The keywords for the exams I sat after a few hours or days of study (speed-studying) required one hundred and fifty to six hundred points in multiple journeys. A friend of mine speed-studied and passed an exam with just thirty keywords. If you have prior knowledge in the subject, have been to lectures or at least read some of the syllabus, you could obviously get top marks without memorising at all. But memorising won't hurt. All it will do is make sure that you can express your knowledge in a clear manner.

Personally, I have passed exams in psychology after just a few days of studying – but I have also failed. Did I write poorly? Unlikely, as half the exam was multiple choice, and I also have a lot of writing experience. Did I understand the questions? Was three days of studying too little to understand the subject? I had no trouble understanding the questions. Reading the syllabus was challenging as there were many difficult and new words and concepts – but with the help of the dictionary I understood the topics. The reason that I failed was mainly poor time management prior to the exam. I didn't stay focused when I read through the material, which resulted in too little 'meat' on the keywords. Only having time to read half the syllabus didn't help either.

No stress

Using Memo gives a fantastic sense of security. It feels like having a notebook with the most important keywords open on your desk during the exam. Exams used to cause a lot of stress – now they cause excitement. Normal rote learning generally only helps for the short-term. By using locations it becomes long-term. Locations also make it easier to revise and significantly improve the effectiveness of revision. It doesn't matter how long it took you to acquire the knowledge – five days instead of five months – as long as it is in your long-term memory in the end.

Oral exams

Memo is even better for oral exams. The exam you read about in the introduction was an oral exam. The method is the same as for written exams. You may have to give a presentation prior to answering questions. Memorise the keywords and give your presentation without looking at notes – it was a revered skill in ancient Greece and still makes a good impression on examiners. The main difference from a written exam is that at the oral exam you will have to recall the keywords quickly. Prior to the exam you should therefore spend some extra time to make sure you have your journeys under control, as this will speed up the recall.

Summary

Trying to pass an exam in a complex subject on just three days of study without any prior knowledge is demanding. But Memo is not just an example of how little time you can spend studying. It is also a method for getting really good marks if you do take the time to study, as well as an argument for never giving up before an exam regardless of how impossible it may look. Make keywords that will remind you of the knowledge you have. Later you create associations for the keywords – as the keywords can be hard to visualise. Create keywords in one study session, and associations in another. This way you focus on one thing at a time. Then you memorise.

Memo everyday

Remembering appointments

You are out driving. The phone rings. How are you supposed to remember the appointment? Or, off the top of your head, if you are free for lunch in two weeks time? The numerical systems are useful to keep your appointments under control. Here are two methods for everyday use.

Weekly schedules

Let us divide a friends house into seven areas or rooms. Each room will represent a weekday. One way to divide the house:

Veranda: Monday

Kitchen: Tuesday

Bedroom: Wednesday

Bathroom: Thursday

Rumpus room: Friday

Hallway: Saturday

Garden: Sunday

The rooms are in order. From the veranda I walk into the kitchen. Like Tuesday is after Monday. I zigzag through the house until I have seven points. We fill the calendar with appointments. You promised Mark to return his tennis racket on Tuesday. To remember that, we think about the kitchen – Tuesday. Create an image that will remind you to return the racket. You could imagine Mark getting eggs out of the fridge and hitting them around the kitchen with the racket. Should be more than enough to remember the deal.

I tend to memorise appointments as I make them. The rooms you use to represent the weekdays can be re-used every week. As old appointments will fade away there is little danger of confusion. Next week, logic should tell you that the tennis racket has already been returned.

Time can also be memorised in the calendar. Use the Single System for the number 0 to 9. In the Alternative Double System we learnt that 10 is Dido, 11 is Pippi Longstocking and 12 is Ian Thorpe. We use these associations to visualise appointments based on time. In the single system 8 is a snowman. I am going to the dentist at 8 am Monday. I imagine a dentist on the veranda. He is extracting a tooth from the snowman. When I later think about my appointments I will see the poor snowman – reminding me that the appointment is at 8. The veranda tells me it is on Monday. Double booking is uncool. So next time someone asks if you are free Monday morning, you won't have to think about it – you will know the answer straight away. My history lectures are every Friday at 10. Dido (person for number 10) is in the rumpus room with the lecturer. They are looking at cow. No wonder I have yet to miss a lecture in auditorium C. The visualisation is reinforced every time you think about it. Eventually you will automatically know when the lecture is without having to think about the cow.

To memorise times like quarter past or half you can use the Alternative Double System with symbols from 00 to 24. At Nine Fifty Sunday night I have to be at the airport to pick up some friends. That is why I see Tiger Woods (person 21) soaping (action 50) the passenger in the garden (Sunday). Think about your schedule when you wake up. That way you will be in complete control of the day's appointments. If you need to memorise a lot of appointments happening more than a week from now you can create a journey of thirty-one points; where every point represents a date.

Agenda

Agenda is a method to use to remember tasks that don't have a special timeframe attached. You are sitting on the toilet. The last piece of paper rolls of the toilet roll. How are you going to remember to buy some more? Where is your diary when you need it the most? Where is the post-it note to write a shopping list? Here is the recipe. You have already made a journey of ten to fifteen points. It may be the hotel room, the veranda, the pool, the vending machine, the reception, the convenience store, the American restaurant and so on.

Lately I have had to do a lot of tasks that have no timeframe other than that I need to do it. That is why I memorise them in the agenda instead of the weekly schedule

1. Get camera fixed
2. Water the flowers
3. Vacuum the car
4. Chop firewood
5. Pay Simon the $50 I owe him from the last poker night
6. Stop playing poker

This is how you could memorise it: Imagine a broken camera in the hotel room. Should be enough to remind me to take it in to get fixed. As I walk on the veranda, flowers as dry as spaghetti crunch under my feet; remember to water the flowers. And so on.

I am still sitting here on the toilet. I've had enough of using coffee filters – I have to remember to buy toilet paper. No problem, lots of free points in the agenda. I go to the seventh point – the American restaurant. The waiter at the restaurant is covered in toilet paper. Of course: crappy American food. Did you notice how easy it was to visualise? The best part about watering the flowers is that we can cross it off the list with an ugly, black pen. We just don't have a list to cross out. Let us throw in a hand grenade instead; we blow up the whole veranda. Bang! The veranda is empty. Ready for the next task the boss throws your way.

Should you need a longer list you can just add points. Or memorise additional items in one point. Put the toilet paper inn with the camera. The method works differently for different people, but there are options. You are still in the toilet. Instead of memorising the toilet paper on the agenda, you pick up the roll and throw it in front of the bathroom door. It will be hard to miss the roll when you walk out the door. Pick it up and don't put it down until you have added it to the traditional shopping list.

Birthdays, anniversaries and other important dates

Monday's Child is Fair of Face;
Tuesday's Child is Full of Grace;
Wednesday's Child is Full of Woe;
Thursday's Child has Far to Go;
Friday's Child is Loving and Giving;
Saturday's Child works Hard for a Living;
The Child that is born on Sunday is Bonny and Blythe and Good in every way.

Divide a house into twelve areas. This house will be your calendar for birthdays, anniversaries and other important dates. Each room or area represents a month. The calendar could start in the study – symbolising January. The next room, the bathroom, is February.

The lounge room, March. The months follow the logical sequence of the rooms; this makes it easier to remember which room represents which month.

January: Study
February: Bathroom
and so on...
September: Hallway
October: Laundry
November: Shed
December: Garage

Jane's birthday is 23 September. Imagine Jane in the hallway, as this is the room for September. To memorise the date we use the action from the Alternative Double System. The action for 23 is to telephone, so we visualise Jane doing just that. Sarah's birthday is 21 October. Visualise Sarah in the Laundry (October). The Laundry is so small that she has to tie up all the clothes to keep them off the floor. To tie is the action for the number 21. Should you wish to remember the year Sarah was born, you simply add the person representing that year. Sarah was born in 1971and the association for 71 is a lion. Sarah is in the laundry trying to tie up the lion. The laundry tells you it is October, the rest will tell you the date and year. If several people have birthdays the same month, you just memorise them in the same room; there is room enough for all of them. Important future events can also be memorised. You are going to a Christening on 13 November. Imagine a miner (person 13) christening the child in the shed.

Memorising manuscripts, speeches and texts

- You want some bacon?
- No, man, I don't eat pork.

To learn a manuscript by heart can be a formidable task. Actors use methods to learn their lines, either consciously or unconsciously. Variants of the link method are quite common. Unfortunately, Memo is not yet well known in Hollywood and actors waste a lot of time. Here are the lines for Vincent (John Travolta) and Jules (Samuel L. Jackson) from a scene in *Pulp Fiction*:

VINCENT: You want some bacon?

Jules: No, man, I don't eat pork.

VINCENT: Are you Jewish?

Jules: No, I ain't Jewish, I just don't dig on swine, that's all.

VINCENT: Why not?

Jules: Pigs are filthy animals. I don't eat filthy animals.

VINCENT: But bacon tastes good, pork chops taste good ...

Jules: Hey, sewer rat may taste like pumpkin pie, but I'd never know 'cause I wouldn't eat the filthy animals. Pigs sleep and root in shit, that's a filthy animal. I don't eat nothin' that ain't got sense enough to disregard its own faeces.

VINCENT: How about a dog? A dog eats its own faeces.

Jules: I don't eat dog either.

VINCENT: Yeah, but do you consider a dog to be a filthy animal?

To memorise Vincent Vega's lines in this scene we need a journey of seven points. Words in bold are keywords to remind us of the rest of the sentence. Before we memorise we create associations from words that are easy to visualise. Then we memorise the associations like we normally do, in a journey.

1. Bacon
2. Jew
3. A man shrugs (Why)
4. Bacon and pork
5. A dog eating his own faeces
6. The dogs is bathing in mud

We have now memorised keywords for each of Vincent's lines. To remember the line perfectly we will have to read through all the lines as few times. This is to know what the keywords tell us. The reason we don't memorise the lines word by word is that it takes too long. And our performance will be slow and jerky. Still, it is no problem to perform the lines perfectly as the keywords will help us remember the rest. With some practice you will be able to recite the lines without having to mentally walk through the journey, although this is neither a pro nor a con.

The same approach can be used for speeches, lectures or other per-formances. In most of these instances you will not need the perfec-tion of the lines above, so you will need less points in the journey. The method has great advantages. First of all you can focus solely on the performance rather than on remembering the lines. Are you giving a speech, or making a presentation, you can keep eye contact and interact with the audience at all times. It will take less time to learn the manuscript and you will need fewer revisions. The con-tents of all manuscripts, speeches and presentation have an order. By saving the text in a journey you will have full control over the order. In addition to lines you can memorise actions or movements, if you are learning a play for example. Learning texts in foreign languages is much easier. And the best part: it is all saved in your long-term memory.

It cannot be emphasised enough how effective Memo is for speeches, manuscripts, lectures and presentations. Even if someone else writes your speech, you create a list of keywords and memorise them in a journey. You will become a speaker of the quality of the great Greeks and Romans of the past.

Honey, where are the keys?

"Oh where, oh where could my keys/wallet/phone/sunglasses/credit card be?"

People often ask for tips on how to remember where they put their keys. Most sensible, obviously, is to always put them in the same spot. Place a bowl on the table in the hallway and put the keys there when you get home. Do it now or forget about it. If you don't have a set place to put them, then my best advice is to throw them on the floor in the middle of the room. Forgetting where you parked or where you put the keys is all about focus or lack thereof. If you where not consciously aware of the action it will be harder to remember it. A well-known method to find a missing item is to go back to where it was last seen; even a thought or idea is often searched for this way – sometimes successfully. One method to remember where you placed something is to do something different when you put it there. If you place your Passport in an unusual place you need to be aware of the action. Try to make the situation unique; only use your thumbs to place the Passport in the drawer. Maybe even say it out loud: "I am placing the Passport in the underwear drawer." This makes the situation unique and you avoid mixing it up with previous placements of the item.

Remembering key points in conversations

You meet Dave and you remember that you have to ask him to borrow his keys before he goes on holidays. Dave starts talking, and by the time you finally get a word in you have forgotten. To avoid this you can visualise; focus on visualising the keys where you are or in a journey. When Dave is done talking, chances are you will actually remember to ask.

Sometimes I also use the journey method to memorise information from the conversation. I memorise keywords in a journey parallel with the conversation. The method is especially useful during a phone conversation where you don't have pen and paper available. Important messages are much easier to remember by visualising them in a journey. You can always write them down later. Tying a point to a finger is an old method. You have probably seen politicians using their fingers to "count" their arguments as they make them. The method is based on tying one argument to each finger. Imagine that you are going to a meeting and have arguments on nuclear power, sewage recycling and council rates to remember. Imagine that you, Homer Simpson-like, dip your thumb in uranium. Imagine a toilet roll around your index finger. Visualise your middle finger wrapped in money. When you get up to talk you think about the keywords you have tied to each finger. You will remember the uranium thumb; so you go through you arguments regarding nuclear power.

Crossing your fingers is a similar method. Should a good point pop into your head mid-debate or mid-conversation, you can cross you fingers to remember the point. If you have to remember something important you can always do the old string trick; tie a string around your finger. It may look a little stupid, but no memory technique is too stupid if what you have to say is important.

It can be painful to forget good ideas and ideas generally pop up when you don't have pen and paper easily accessible. You can use the orange method, put something on the ground or move something, while thinking about the idea. Or you can use a journey. Visualise the idea in one or more points in the journey. Did you come up with a brilliant idea to manufacture blow-up dartboards? If you use the journey to your primary school you can imagine the stairs, the first point in the journey. There is a blow-up dartboard on the stairs. Maybe you even jump up and down on it, as movement is easier to remember. A lot of the ideas for this book popped into my head while I was having a shower, riding my bike or somewhere else where I couldn't just pull out pen and paper. So instead of losing the ideas, I memorised them in a journey.

Jokes, riddles, quotes and stories

A lady goes to her mother's funeral. At the funeral she meets a man she doesn't know. She thinks he's the one and falls head over heals in love. The man leaves the funeral without giving her his name or number. Nobody knows him and she simply cannot find out who he is. A few days later she kills her sister. What is her motive for the murder?

Read the solution in the next paragraph. You hardly need a method to remember it, if one riddle is all you know. But by using Memo you can quickly create a large folder of jokes, riddles, quotes and stories in you long-term memory. To remember a lot of riddles or jokes, you should memorise them in a journey. Create keywords for each riddle and memorise. The keywords for this riddle could be *the dream guy* and *coffin*. Visualise these at one point in the journey.

The solution to the riddle: She killed her sister in the hope that the guy would show up for the funeral. This riddle is used in the US as a test to see if you are crazy. It is claimed that psychopaths and mass murderers solve it straight away, as their thinking in different. To them, the riddle is too simple. Relax – a riddle is just a riddle.

Here is a fascinating way to use your memory. Think about a wish. Don't say it out loud – just think about it. Say the answers to the following questions out loud (or write them down, as I am not there to remember the answers for you). Rate these animals from one to five, based on which animal you like the most: Monkey, Cow, Horse, Sheep and Tiger. What to you think about cats - What's your view on them? What do you think about dogs? What about coffee – what do you think about when you heard the word coffee? Who, of people you know, do you think about when you hear the word Yellow? Who do you think about with Orange? Red? White? Green? What is your favourite number (1 to 31)? What is your favourite weekday?

Ok, this is how you rate your life: the animal rated number one is most important, five the least. Monkey is money; Cow is career; Horse is family; Sheep is love; and Tiger is pride. What you said about cats is how you see yourself. You think you partner is what you said about dogs. You enjoy sex like you enjoy coffee. The yellow person will never forget you. Orange person is your best friend. Red is your true love. White person is your soul mate. You want to fly to the moon with green person. Your wish from the start will be fulfilled the next time your favourite weekday falls on the date of your favourite number. So watch out!

It may be a childish play, but it is a perfect example on how to use Memo in practice. Create a journey of sixteen points and memorise one keyword at each point. The first image can be a present (think about a wish), the second a monkey. Then cow, horse, sheep, tiger, cat, dog, coffee and ocean. Use associations for the colours: a yellow submarine, an orange and a rose. When you have memorised the entire list you can ask the questions straight from your memory. You can use the Single System to memorise which animals people prefer. If the person says tiger is 1 and horse is 2, you visualise, at the appropriate point in the journey, a pole with the tiger and a swan on the horse's back. When you ask about the cat, you memorise their answer at the point where the cat already is. When all the questions have been answered you can recall the order of priorities, tell them what they think about themselves, who their soul mate is and when their wish will come true.

Phone numbers

Americans have letters on the buttons of their home phones, just like we have on our mobiles. They are good at creating words from phone numbers to make them easier to remember. To get baseball tickets in Philadelphia you could just call 1-800-PHILLY-TIX – pushing the buttons with the corresponding letter on it.

We can use the same principle to make it easier for other people to remember our own phone number.

As you can see from your mobile, your can make the words *girl power* for the phone number 4475 76937. Turn on your dictionary and type away. Unfortunately there are no letters for 0 and 1, but you can create words from parts of the number. 9191 4263 could be 9191 HAND. You will have to be a little lucky to find good words, but if you can it will make it a lot easier for people to remember as it is much more visual. Use the same method to create associations for pin numbers and passwords.

You can use the Alternative Double System to make the phone numbers you wish to remember more visual. Divide the number into two digit chunks. The two first numbers become a person, the next two the action. You are trying to remember the number 3587

9741. Imagine an Eskimo (person 35) falling (action 87). George Lucas (person 97) riding (action 41). To ensure storage in your long-term memory you should visualise the images in two points in a journey; for example the front door and the parking lot: Imagine the Eskimo falling out the front door. George Lucas riding in the parking lot. Should you know where the person lives, the best place to store his phone number is their house. You have to remember Alister's phone number. Imagine the action taking place in his lounge room, or the garden. His study is also a suitable storage place. Save the numbers of your colleagues in the office, your family in your house and friends' numbers in their houses.

000 is a number you should already know. If you don't, memorise it now. If could also be smart to memorise the non-emergency numbers for your local police, hospital, fire brigade and other important services. Generally these services try to have a number that is easy to remember; they may even have similar numbers. For example the Police Assistance number is 131 444, the Emergency Roadside assistance is 131 111 and the Poison information centre is 131 126. The police station serves as a natural place for storing the police number – the car the obvious place for the RAA. As you have several numbers that start with 131, you only have to memorise the digits that are different, in this case the last three. You can use a combination of the double and Single System to memorise the numbers. This is how you can visualise the Police assistance: Robert Redford (44) sailing (4). You have already decided on the police station as the location for the number, so imagine Robert Redford sailing in the police station.

The Triple System may be even better for memorising important numbers, for example:

- 111 = nan -> nanny
- 126 = nec -> neck

Use the associations to create wacky images to remember phone numbers. Visualise the images in logical places and make sure you can really see them in your mind. If you call the police assistance number 131 444, you will be automatically connected to your nearest police station. If you want to memorise the entire number you can divide the number into blocks of two: 13 14 44 and memorise it using the Double System. Or keep it at 131 444 and memorise it using the Triple System. Soon you will have a great, big phonebook in your mind.

Job interviews

Nothing is worse than walking out of a job interview and then suddenly remembering important information you forgot to talk about. In this age of behavioural questions it is even more important to think about possible questions and answers prior to the interview. That is why you should memorise important keywords in a journey of ten or more points. Think about how you want to portrait yourself. What are your positive skills and relevant competencies? Why should they hire you? Some interviewers will even ask you to list, say, three strengths and three weaknesses. It is times like these you will be glad you thought through the answers beforehand rather than a 30 second "ehhhh...". With your keywords safely stored in your long-term memory you can leave the fear of forgetting behind and concentrate on showing them why you are the right person for the job. What is the biggest challenge you have faced? They all seem to want to know about a time you had to deal with a difficult customer – what happened, how did you deal with it and what was the outcome? Why do you want to work for this company? And, importantly, what do you know about the firm? Saying that you have looked through their website simply won't do. People that show an interest in the company impress interviewers. So make sure you memorise a few keywords about the firm and, if you can find the information, about the interviewers.

Write down what you want to remember and visualise it. How you utilise the information is up to you. The interview will not be about trying to remember, but about performance. You can see the keywords in the journey. The weight comes off your shoulders and you can relax. Try to have an empty journey ready in your mind; save important information you are told during the interview and write down the key information afterwards. Remembering what was said in the interview can be critical if you have to come back for another interview later on.

Be better at sports by using your memory

Most sports consist of a sequence of movements you will have to perform to get the desired result. The best effect is achieved once movements have become automatic. To get there you will have to go through a process to learn the movements. I will never claim to be a golf expert – but even in golf there are several things to consider to hit the ball perfectly:

1. Grip
2. Clubface aim
3. Ball position
4. Posture
5. Backswing

6. Top of backswing
7. Downswing
8. Impact
9. Follow through
  (O'Brien: 1993, p 117)

No, I am not saying that you should think through the entire list every time, but rather memorise the list to keep track of the things to consider. Earlier in the book your read that dance steps and combinations can be memorised. Another way to memorise the combinations is to visualise them at points in a journey instead of visualising their names. That is, you visualise the moves you do in the dance. You can also use this method to learn how to juggle. Imagine the different tricks in a journey. The purpose is to remember all the different tricks you know. The name of the trick can be memorised at the same point or its own point.

Some athletes memorise the actual plays of the game. A well known example of this is when the Japanese volleyball coach Matsudaira called a new setter into his office after his first practice: "Tell me about all the sets you made and why you choose those options." Nekoda could not, so he learnt memory methods to ensure that he could in the future. They found that the techniques were especially useful for scouting the opposition. The Japanese volleyball team later became Olympic champions. Few readers will have much use of memorising volleyball, but as we can see Memo can be used for a lot of different things; sports included. The short story: you can memorise sporting plays using a combination of journeys and numerical systems.

Parking

You should not have too much trouble remembering where you parked your car in Coober Pedy, but having read the following advice in a memory improvement book I would like to offer some tips:

> "Parking garages often have letters or similar codes that it pays to register."

Of course it pays to register where you have parked. This, however, does not necessarily give you better memory - which is what the book promises. You should rather use the effective methods of location and visualisation. You have parked in section E of the car park. Maybe noticing the letter will be enough to find your car – but for now the E is just floating around in your mind. You should place the information in a location to secure proper recall. The car seat is a prime location; the phonetic alphabet and the Single System are perfect for memorising where you parked. Visualise an Ecco-shoe in the driver's seat (Echo is E in the phonetic alphabet). Maybe the shoe is jumping around and kicking the brake pedal? Hours later, when you are tired and trying to find your car, you can think: Where did I store the information? In the driver's seat. What's in there? An Ecco-shoe. Ecco because I parked in the E section.

If you park in the same car park every day and in different sections, you may mix previous images with the latest one. There are two solutions. One, you can link the letter to the weekday. If you park in section G on Thursday, you can imagine Thor with a golf club (instead of the hammer). Golf is G in the phonetic alphabet. Friday you parked in section C; imagine **Charlie** Chaplin eating French **Fries** (Charlie is C in the phonetic alphabet).

The other option is to memorise the letters in the weekly schedule. You can memorise images for the day's parking sport in one of the seven rooms. If the veranda is Monday and you're parked in section C, you can imagine Charlie Chaplin out there. Generally it should be enough to visualise the phonetic letter in the driver's seat. If you start mixing them you can always try the other methods.

The same method can be used for parking in streets and parking lots. If you park in Blue Gum Ave you can imagine a gumtree growing out of the seat and through the roof. If you parked by No 8 Blue gum Ave you can visualise a snowman on top of the gumtree – maybe it is even a snow gum? You can always use other landmarks to help remembering where you parked. If you parked by a rubbish container, you can imagine trash in the car. A bit filthy maybe, but you won't forget.

Directions

She rolls down the window to ask. "Well, first you turn right into Manning Road, then left at the second intersection. Turn right and right again at the roundabout, then left twice. Something like that."

Remembering directions can be difficult. If your have to make ten turns it will be almost impossible to remember when to turn right. It all has to happen in the correct order: we can memorise it in a journey. Here are some made up directions:

1. Turn left onto the main road
2. Make a right in the roundabout
3. Drive through three tunnels
4. Turn right at the Shell petrol station
5. Continue for four kilometres
6. Drive past the church
7. Go straight through the stop-light
8. Turn left into Bishop Street
9. Turn into Fox Street
10. The Bowling alley is on the right. It is green.

It is a challenging trip, but by no means unrealistic. I have already decided that a roundabout = a steering wheel; straight ahead = compass; stoplight = cheese; and tunnel = a barrel. Left = Communist and right = Rainbow. We visualise an action at each point in the journey. Here is a journey to memorise the directions:

1. Hotel room
2. Bathroom
3. Hallway

And so on until you get to point 10, laundry.

First you turn left into the main road. Imagine the Communist in your hotel room. No need to stay there. To your great surprise you find a rainbow rising over the steering wheel in the bathtub. Turn right at the roundabout. In the hallway you have to crawl through three barrels. Drive through three tunnels. Continue until you have memorised them all. The tenth, and last, point could be like this:

In the laundry a green bowling ball rolls down the rainbow. The bowling alley is on the right (rainbow). The house is green.

The method may seem cumbersome, but you will get there first and won't need to fiddle with the map while you drive.

Numbers and letters in general

There are times when it is not necessary to memorise numbers, letters, codes and passwords in journeys. Yet it is easy to forget the number on the bus you were supposed to catch. Here are some practical examples on memorising numbers and letters.

Examples from the Single System

You are told to turn the stove down to 4 when the rice is boiling. To improve the chance you will remember 4 you can imagine a sailboat (4 in the Single System) in the pot. The image only takes a second to create and the active thinking significantly improves the possibility that you will remember. Your train departs from platform 9. If you have a tendency to forget this, you can imagine an axe or whatever else you have created as you image for the number 9. You filled up with petrol on pump number 2, but by the time you have bought all your food and drinks inside, you have forgotten. Next time you fill up at pump number 2, you can imagine a swan at the end of the hose.

Examples from the Alternative Double System (ADS)

Are you buying 24 eggs? Think about Theodore Roosevelt. He is the association for the number 24 in the Alternative Double System. You could also use the Single System and think about a swan in a sailboat. I prefer using the ADS. Theodore Roosevelt is one thing. A swan and a sailboat are two things to remember. Your brother calls and says it's Aunt Brenda's 68th Birthday and you have to call and congratulate. Imagine a cat (68 in the ADS) for a second and you will remember how old your aunt is. The postcode 4345 can be visualised by imagining a reptile (43) brushing its teeth (action for 45). To remember if you have taken your pills or vitamins you can use the Alternative Double System. Today is the 17th. Visualise Ivan Lendl building a tower with the pills (person 18 and his action - building). If you would rather use the Double System-system, you can imagine a nomad (18) playing with the pills tomorrow. Only creating associations for the numbers activate less of your long-term memory than for creating locations and journeys. Putting the images in a location, like the sailboat in the pot, will strengthen the memory even more. Generally this would be information that you only want to remember for a few hours; a quick image is enough.

Examples from the Triple System

You have to turn the oven to 200 degrees. Think about the Triple System:

2 = T, 0 = oo, 0 = th. 200 = tooth. Imagine the tooth in the oven.

Make it a habit to memorise the number on your taxi. You catch taxi number 289 in Fiji. 289 = tig. The vowel is pronounced as the i in high, so we get tiger. Imagine a tiger in the back seat. The chance of getting your forgotten mobile back have at least not decreased. Did the taxi number have a letter too? M289. M is Mike in the phonetic alphabet. Maybe Mike Tyson and the tiger are having a fight in the back seat? But how big is the island, really? All the taxis probably have the same letter. Drop the letter and focus on the number. Memorising is often about removing useless information. You put the novel aside having read page 195. In the Triple System 195 is n o s = nose. Imagine the nose on the book.

Examples from the phonetic alphabet

Imagine that you are meeting someone at exit F. You could think of a fox, as Foxtrot is the code for F in the phonetic alphabet. The phonetic alphabet is useful for all memorising that involves letters. Are you sitting in seat 26 D on the plane you can imagine Tom Cruise (26 in the ADS) showing off his Deltoids in the seat. He is probably showing off before his next movie premiere. To maximise recall you should place the image in a location. A quick visualisation is often enough. We can also use the phonetic alphabet to remember single letters. Lori has invited you over for coffee and cakes at L28 Eden Street. Imagine a Taxi driver (28) riding a Lama (L) around the Garden of Eden.

Vitamin D. It is good for something, but what? Vitamin D and omega-3 are important for the brain, heart and immune system. Imagine a weight lifter with massive Deltoids. On one shoulder he's got a tattoo of a heart - on the other a tattoo of a brain. Imagine him lifting an immigrant (association for immune).

Music

Some can remember lyrics, chords and notes without trouble. Others have to actively use memory methods. Lyrics can be memorised just like manuscripts. Guitar chords can be memorised using journeys – but here is an alternative method. The Chord chart for The house of the rising sun goes like this:

Am, C, D, F
Am, C, E, E
Am, C, D, F
Am, E
Am, C, D, F
Am, E, Am, E

To remember the order we can use the story method. We create a story of the chords to remind us of the order. Am and C reminds me of Am Car. So imagine a large, petrol guzzling American car driven by Dawn Fraser (D, F) passing by. We have compressed four chords into one image. Next, another Am Car drives past - this time driven by Ernie Els (the golfer - E, E). Every new chord is followed by the Am Car with Dawn Fraser (Am, C, D, F). Then a priest yells AmEn! (Am and E). The Am Car with Dawn Fraser (Am, C, D, F) drives by again before two priests shouting AmEn, AmEn! (Am, E, Am, E). Silly? Maybe, but it works.

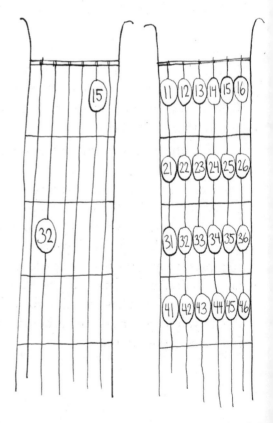

Playing the guitar

We can use the Alternative Double System to memorise chords. We name all the areas on the neck based on the placement of the string and fret. Create an association for Cadd9. I imagine dogs, as 'CaNe' means dog in Italian. Fret 1, string 5 becomes 15. Fret 3, string 2 turns into 32. Fish is 15 in the ADS, 32 is ET. Visualise the fish betting (ET's action) on some dogs (CaNe).

The B Chord looks like this. Barre on the second fret. A barre can be memorised as zero. We get 2 (second fret) and 0 (barre) = 20. The other fingers are placed in fret four, on strings three, four and five.

4 (fourth fret) 3 (third string) = 43
4 (fourth fret) 4 (fourth string) = 44
4 (fourth fret) 5 (fifth string) = 45.

Imagine a bar. The bar is the association for the B chord. In the bar you see a tomboy (person 20) reading (action 43). Robert Redford (person 44) is brushing his teeth (action 45) next to them.

Locate the chords in different locations – this makes it easier to find them when you need them. For example visualise the D Chord in the dining room. Although the images you learned here should be enough when you suddenly go blank whilst trying to impress some girl while backpacking around Europe. Once you have practiced a few times, the chords will become so automatic that you won't even have to think about Robert Redford and fish. Should you forget one or more chords, you can always go back and find them in your mind.

Names and faces

People often ask me how I remember decks of cards, keywords for exams and how I can possibly memorise a thousand numbers in an hour. By far the most questions are about how to remember names and faces. Or, to be correct, just names. We remember faces but struggle with names. We are wired to remember faces; our ancestors had to be able to instantly distinguish friend from foe. There is, however, no logic between looks and names – you have to recall the name from the great beyond or use methods. Several methods for remembering names exist, both for use in competitions and everyday life. The methods have pros and cons, depending on the situation. Most importantly though, is to *pay attention* when people are introduced. Quite often we are so focused on our own name that we completely miss the name of the person we just met. We can neither remember nor forget a name we never picked up in the first place – the method we use to remember it won't matter. Repeat the name of the person you were introduced to, just to make sure you got it right. Use the name often in conversations, like when asking questions, to make it automatic.

Here and now

You ring the doorbell at a friend's house. A girl you have never met before opens the door. Her name is Angela. Imagine an angel in the doorway. Should you forget her name by the next time you meet, you will know where to look: the first place you met her. You use the effective location method. Knowing where in you mind you should look for information is a great advantage for correct recall. The method, however, has its limitations. Storing the ten players on your new cricket team on the pitch is too complicated. The method is most suitable when meeting a few people or when used in combination with other methods.

Using Celebrities

Does a person remind you of a celebrity or friend? Small similarities, like the same nose, are enough. You just met John. He looks like Pete Sampras. You associate Sampras with tennis. Imagine a tennis court – this will be your location for the name. Imagine John Howard waving a racket on the tennis court. The next time you meet John, you see that he looks a bit like Pete Sampras – so the name must be stored on the tennis court. On the tennis court you see John Howard. The thought process is amazingly quick: "Hey John!" If you run into John often enough you won't have to check out the tennis court every time; the name becomes automatic. The location secures the recall until you know you have learnt the name.

This may sound complicated, but it is effective. The method is simple: you look for characteristics that reminds you of someone you know – be it friend or famous. You then choose a natural location to save the name and visualise an image for the name. The name is saved in a set location, in the long-term memory. Using the long-term memory is the smartest thing you can do.

You just met Cathy. She looks a bit like the checkout girl at Coles. Imagine a cat (association for Cathy) at the checkout. Want to remember her last name too? Pennell. Visualise the checkout girl writing an L on the cat with a pen. As you can see, the image you visualise to remember the name can be someone else you know, an item you associate with the name, or both. You are introduced to Don. His hair reminds you of Richard from primary school. Imagine Richard's house or the classroom and visualise Donald Duck there. Quack, quack. You have probably managed to forget what someone job or degree is, even if you have asked them every time you have seen them during the past year. We save the information about Don in Richard's house. It is a big house, so there is plenty of room for more information. Don is a medical student. Dress him up in a coat and a stethoscope. You will naturally remember a lot, but there are virtually no limits to how much you can memorise.

"Are you coming over to Wombat Street for a poker night tonight?" Don asks. You can probably guess where you should save the address. Imagine a wombat trying to bite Donald Duck's tail. Later in the conversation Don tells you he has got problems with his knee. Want to ask Don at a later date how his knee is doing? Imagine Donald whacking his knee with a hammer. That must be allowed – after all, he is studying to become a doctor.

Action

Action is a method where you imagine the person you met doing an action that you closely associate with the name. New guy at footy-practice: Tony. The name makes me think of a Taekwondo guy I know, so I imagine the person doing kung-fu stuff. The method is essentially based on linking the new Tony with the actions of the Tony I already know.

This method is a little risky because you have not placed the association in a location. Quite often, however, the place you met the person in will be a good enough location. Don't be afraid to use the method and strengthen the image by repeating it until the name becomes automatic.

To memorise an entire name you can imagine the person performing an action. If you meet Eileen Harris you can visualise her with hair in her eye. Unusual images are easier to remember. You meet Justin Hayden. Make the person into a subject, the first name into an action and the surname into an item: Imagine the man making juice (Justin) out of hay.

Multiple names

Being introduced to several new people at once is a massive challenge. It is often hectic and you barely have time to introduce yourself. One method is to memorise the names in a journey. Greer is the first person to introduce herself. Memorise a Greer you know already or an association for the name at the first point in the journey. Memorise the names in the order they are introduced. The challenge with this method is that you are unlikely to meet the same people in the same order later and you have not memorised the name in relation to their face. At least you have memorised the names.

You can also use the here-and-now technique when you are introduced to several people. Visualise an association or celebrity where the person in question is standing or sitting. Charlotte sits at the head of the table. Imagine a shallot (onion) at the head of the table. The method is surprisingly effective. Your natural memory is an expert in remembering who sat where. Chances are good that – now that you have memorised the name in a journey or the person's location – you will link the right name to the right face.

About associations

All the previous methods are based on associating the name with an item or someone with the same name; you imagine John Howard when you meet John, or a cat for Cathy. If you just met Alexandra and don't know anyone else with the same name, you can think about some guy you know named Alexander. The image will be easy to recall and you will know she's not Alexander.

Are you trying to remember the surname Hanson, you can image some hens. It is unlikely you will mix it up with similar names, unless you compete in memory championships. Should you meet a Jackson, you can imagine a burger (Hungry Jacks). The point is that your association need not be perfect and the first association that pops into you mind is usually the best.

Balding-Bill

This technique is based on someone's unique features. You just met Michael – he is wearing glasses. To remember his name you notice that a microphone has replaced his glasses. What if Michael gets contacts? Isn't this a poor method when appearances change? We all struggle to recognise people and the method's got nothing to do with recognition. Recognition relates to our ability to observe. If you have visualised well enough, you will remember Michaels' name even if he gets contact lenses. The challenge is the lack of location. So why not place Michael and the microphone at the music store?

Unique features can easily be combined with other methods. Noticing unusual clothing may help. Normally, it is unique features as well as similarity to others that make us remember people in the first place.

Summary

Some of these methods require you to memorise crazy images – but what's in your mind is nobody's business. Remembering their name will be greatly appreciated.

- Repeat the name
- Use a method to store the name
- Use the name straight away
- Think through or write down the names of new people you met today

Memory tricks and competitions

A man in a black coat walks towards us. He asks if we want to attend his memory improvement seminar.

"Maybe," we reply.

I am visiting a friend doing study abroad in Bologna, Italy. Eric, his girlfriend Mila and I are on our way to the university.

"I will show you how good I am," the man says. "Tell me thirty numbers!"

We quickly give him thirty numbers to write down. "Ok, that's enough!" he says. "How long do you think it will take me to memorise them all?"

"All day," Eric says.

"Ten hours," is Mila's guess.

"Twenty minutes," I say.

The guy smiles and asks Eric to time him.

"Finished!"

"One minute and ten seconds!"

The guy scratches his chin and recalls all thirty numbers in the correct order.

"Cool! Could I try?" I ask.

The man gives me a funny look. "Sure, go ahead!"

"I'll try something different. Read out one number per second and I will try to remember the correct order," I say.

The guy reads out and writes down one number per second.

"Uno, quattro, sette, nove, uno, uno, tre ..."

Thirty numbers in all and it was time for recall. His face grows longer for each number I recall. People stop to watch, completely quiet. I remember all the numbers. "Here, take a flyer" he says. He does not seem too happy. Grinning we keep walking towards the university. Over our shoulder we can see the man gesticulating to other men in black coats.

It is very rare to come across a situation where you can surprise people this way and in memory competitions you really have to be good to utterly impress the other competitors. Every year there are World Championships, National Championships and other memory competitions. One of the most popular events is to memorise a deck of cards.

Memorising a deck of cards

To remember a deck of cards you will have to prepare two things: a method to make the cards visual and a method to remember the order. The best method for remembering the order is through a journey. Pure and simple. The best method for visualising the cards is a matter of choice and taste. Some use a person as the association for each card. For example, Zorro is Jack of Spades, and Queen of Hearts is Delta Goodrem because they look a little like the cards. Using this method you will need a journey of 52 points to remember the order of 52 people (cards). This is a safe method if you know your journeys well. You can also memorise two people at each point and use a journey of only 26 points. Others prefer to have both a person and an action as the association for each card. Zorro is Jack of Spades; his action is fencing. Queen of Hearts is

Delta Goodrem; her action is to sing. Should the first card be Jack of Spades followed by the Queen of Hearts then visualise Zorro singing. This was you can save two cards at one point. During recall you translate the person and action back to the corresponding card. Jack of Spades and Queen of Hearts. In order to memorise a deck of cards you will need to know 52 people and 52 actions and have a journey of 26 points.

It may be easier to use items as associations instead of people and actions. Six of Clubs could be a shoe – for no special reason. Or you can use the associations based on letters – like in the Double System. All Spades starts with a S, seven is L in the Double System. Seven of Spades become SL – slave. Memorise two words at each point. You can even memorise three words at each point – but make sure you have a system for where you put the first, second and third word.

As I often memorise numbers I use 52 of the people and actions from the Alternative Double System to memorise decks of cards. This way I cut down the number of systems to keep track of. I actually made the associations for the cards first and then transferred them to the Alternative Double System (ADS) later. Thus, there is no need to learn the entire Alternative Double System before you try to memorise a deck of cards. Translating the cards to letters can create the person for the association. All spades become words starting with S. The number two could be t. Two of Spades - ST - starfish. Eight of spades - Sa - Saddam. You can also create their actions based on the letters. Starfish – stab. Saddam – sailing.

Remember, it will take time to make the associations automatic regardless of whether you transfer the associations from the ADS, the Double System or create random associations. Try learning a few at a time, like all hearts from Ace, 2, 3 to 10, instead of attempting to learn them all in one go. Then try all the hearts and all the spades. As your associations become automatic you will memorise the deck faster. You should therefore have several journeys you swap between if you attempt more than one deck a day. Journeys of 26 or 52 can be a bit strange in the beginning but they too will become automatic once you have used them a few times.

There are really only 52 things to remember. The biggest obstacle is learning the associations properly. In the chapter on journeys you easily remembered both ten and fourteen items. Add details to your images to improve the quality of you memorisation. Make sure you really see what is happening. Add sound effects, smells and touch to the images.

There are two ways to look through the deck of cards. One is to hold the deck in one hand and put one card at a time on the table. Or you can hold the deck in both hands and push each card to the other hand. Like a fan. Moving the cards quickly while memorising will improve your speed. In the beginning you will have to put up with a lot of mistakes but soon your recall will be perfect. The recall itself usually takes longer than the memorising, but in competition only your memorising is against the stopwatch.

Andi Bell holds the official world record in memorising a deck of cards: 31.16 seconds with perfect recall at the World Memory Championships in 2006. My personal best, during practice, is 43 seconds. If the task is to memorise several decks of cards then the rules say that you get 52 points for each deck that is correctly recalled and written down. One mistake gives you 26 points for that deck; two mistakes are zero points. In 2004 I memorised and recalled 162 cards perfectly – three decks and six cards – in ten minutes. In the World Memory Championships there is an event called one-hour cards – memorise, correctly, the most decks of cards in one hour. Ben Pridmore perfectly recalled 27 decks of cards - 1404 cards – in 2006. The limit for what is possible is much higher. Other competitors have managed 28 decks in practice and both Ben and Andi Bell have memorised 35 decks – 1820 cards – during practice. Read more about other records in *Profiles and world records*.

Blackjack

In the early 1990s Dominic O'Brien made stacks of money memorising the cards in Blackjack. On average he made £1000 a day. O'Brien was blacklisted because he made money in the long run – you are not supposed to do this, as "the house always wins." So he travelled to new casinos and beat their Blackjack tables. Now his desk drawer is full of eviction notices from casinos all over the world. I will not give you false hopes for easy money. Times have changed and the casinos are aware of people like Dominic. Being blacklisted at one casino will get you blacklisted at a lot of others at the same time. They also use four to eight decks instead of one. Once you have memorised half a deck or a whole deck, the dealer will shuffle the cards. It may be hard, but if you are good and willing to practice there is still a possibility to beat the house in Blackjack. At least you now have the best method for memorising the cards.

How to always win make-a-match

You have probably played the game Make-a-match. The cards are layed on a table face down. On the back of the cards there are figures; two cards for each figure. Player number one will turn over two cards, keep them if they are alike, or put them back face down if they are not. The aim is to remember where identical figures are placed when you see one identical to a card you have already seen. If the figures on the two cards you turn over are identical, you keep the cards and continue to turn new ones over. The winner collects the most cards. Use a journey to visualise the placement of the figures you have seen. If the other player turns over the two cards top left, you can memorise them in the first two points in the journey. The challenge is when cards are turned over randomly. If this happens you will also have to remember the figures location.

Let us say that we play with thirty cards – fifteen pairs of figures. The cards are placed in a grid with five rows and six columns. The first card turned over is at the bottom right. The figure is a telephone. To memorise where the telephone is, we use the Alternative Double System. The phone is in row five, column six – position 56. Visualise the telephone with either the person or the action for 56 at the first point of the journey. The person for 56 in the ADS is Simon Crean. Imagine Simon talking on the phone at the first point. The next card is a camel. Row three, column two – position 32. Visualise ET (person 32) riding a camel. Your turn. You turn over a parrot in row four, column five – position 45. Visualise a parrot along with the association for 45 at the third point.

The fifth card you turn over another telephone in the middle. You have already seen Simon Crean on the phone, so just turn over position 56 and score your first point.

The journey tells you nothing about the location of the figures. We use the location to store them because it is not enough to just imagine Simon Crean talking on the phone when you have several figures to keep track of. The journey ensures that you visualise instead of just thinking about it. The advantage of the method is that you always know which cards have been turned over. It is also great brain exercise. After a while you can play with one hundred cards just to make it more challenging.

Alternative method

You can create a separate location for each card if you have not learnt the Alternative Double System yet. Store them in one or more rooms you know very well. Store the first three rows in the lounge room, the last three in the kitchen. The figure at the bottom left corner is a heart. Visualise this at the bottom left of the kitchen. Maybe it is the blender. The card in position 23 is a car. Visualise that in the centre of the lounge room, as the first three rows are memorised there and the card is in the middle of the group. When the second heart is turned over I look for the other heart in the two rooms. I find it in the blender at the bottom left of the kitchen. You can now collect both hearts. The recipe to remember games obviously varies as much as the games themselves, but generally a combination of visualisation and location wins.

Which day of the week where you born?

"14 December 1917?"

"Friday!"

You may have seen people on TV that can work out the day of the week of years past. First of all: You don't walk around remembering the weekdays for the entire century. You learn a formula that you can use to calculate the day of the week in seconds. There are several methods. Key to them all is that memory is necessary to be able to calculate the answers. The most common methods are to memorise the moon phases or formulas for which weekday was the first of the month and then calculate the rest based on that. These methods are most suitable if you have nothing else to do.

First I will describe the formula for the method – to show you how easy it is – then show you how to learn it. All you need is to add and subtract. Note that the formula is based on Monday, not Sunday, being the first day of the week. On www.oby.no/au you find a formula for Sunday.

Which day of the week was the 1st of July 1932?

The formula is based on adding numbers. The first number is the date, in this case 1. Then we add the value for the month. This is not a logical value, but a value you have to remember. July is 0. We then add the value for the year. This is also a value you have to remember to be able to calculate the weekday.

The year 1932 has the value 4. We add 1 (date) + 0 (month) + 4 (year) and get 5. The number in the answer is the day of the week. 1 July 1932 was a Friday.

Date + value for the month + value for the year = weekday

Thus, working out the weekday is a combination of memory and easy maths. We have to remember the values for twelve months and a hundred years. Fortunately there are easy ways to memorise this. The value for January is 1; no need to memorise this, as we know January is the first month. The value for February is 4. Memorise that 4 belongs to February. Perhaps you could imagine a feverish (February) person in a sailboat (4 in the Single System). March is also 4. Imagine soldiers marching with the sailboat with the feverish sailor. Memorise the rest by using the Single System and associations for the months.

January: 1	May: 2	September: 6
February: 4	June: 5	October: 1
March: 4	July: 0	November: 4
April: 0	August: 3	December: 6

The years we memorise by using the Alternative Double System and locations. The value for 1932 is 4. Years can have a value from 0 to 6. We can therefore memorise the years in groups. Create seven locations to store the years in. All years with the value 0, I have memorised in the garden.

Years with the value 0:
1901, 1907, 1912, 1918, 1929, 1935, 1940, 1946, 1957, 1963, 1968, 1974, 1985, 1991 and 1996.

To remember that the years I come across in the garden have the value zero you should first visualise a ball in the garden. Ball is 0 in the Single System. You can then visualise the years in the garden using the Alternative Double System. 01 is (Hercule) Poirot; 07 is Osama bin Laden. To make it easier to remember the people you could visualise their actions too. Imagine Poirot oiling Osama bin Laden in the garden. By the outdoor table Ian Thorpe is biting (12) Idi Amin (18). Continue like this until you have memorised all the years.

Decided on locations and memorise the years using the ADS. For example, years with the value 1 you could memorise in the attic, or another suitable place. Remember to visualise the figure for the value 1.

Years with the value 1:
1902, 1913, 1919, 1924, 1930, 1941, 1947, 1952, 1958, 1969, 1975, 1980, 1986 and 1997.

Years with the value 2:
1903, 1908, 1914, 1925, 1931, 1936, 1942, 1953, 1959, 1964, 1970, 1981, 1987, 1992 and 1998.

Value 3:

1909, 1915, 1920, 1926, 1937, 1943, 1948, 1954, 1965, 1971, 1976, 1982, 1993 and 1999.

Value 4:

1904, 1910, 1921, 1927, 1932, 1938, 1949, 1955, 1960, 1966, 1977, 1983, 1988 and 1994.

Value 5:

1905, 1911, 1916, 1922, 1933, 1939, 1944, 1950, 1961, 1967, 1972, 1978, 1989 and 1995.

Value 6:

1900, 1906, 1917, 1923, 1928, 1934, 1945, 1951, 1956, 1962, 1973, 1979, 1984 and 1990.

Which day of the week was 3 March 1907?

We set up the equation: 3 (date) + 4 (soldiers marching with the boat) + 0 (because Osama bin Laden was being oiled in the garden where all the 0 value years are). The answer is 7 - Sunday.

It will be necessary to repeat the memorising of the years to ensure perfect recall. As you may have noticed, the answer will sometimes be 0. The weekday is then Sunday. The number could also be more than seven. If the number is more than seven we have to subtract the largest number that can be divided by seven to get seven or less; subtract seven, fourteen, twenty-one or twenty eight. If the date is 24 July 1989 you have to subtract 21 from the date to get a number of seven or less. 24 less 21 is 3. Add 0 for July and 5 for 1989. The answer is 8. Subtract seven and get 1. 24 July 1989 was a Monday.

Which day of the week was 1 January 1950?

1 (date) + 1 (January's value) + 5 (the value for 1950) = 7 = Sunday.

Which day of the week was D-Day 6 June 1944?

6 (date) + 5 (value for the month of June) = 11. To make the calculations easier we subtract seven straight away. 11 less 7 = 4. We take the value 4 and add 5 (1944's value) = 9. Subtract seven and the answer is 2. D-Day 6 June 1944 was a Tuesday. You should always subtract numbers that are dividable by seven as soon as the sum is more than seven. This makes it easier to solve the equation.

Wonder if the Chernobyl accident 26 April 1986 happened on a Monday?

26 less 21 is 5 (date) + 0 (April) + 1 (1986) = 6. The accident happened on a Saturday.

Calculating the weekdays of a leap year requires a steady hand. We get an extra day 29 February. We therefore have to subtract 1 from the answer if the date is before 1 March. Which day of the week was 16 February in the leap year 1960?

16 less 14 is 2 (date) + 4 (February) + 4 = 10. Subtract seven and get 3. As 1960 was a leap year we have to subtract 1. The weekday was 2, a Tuesday.

1904, 1908, 1912, etc, were leap years. Note that 1900 was not a leap year. Years marking a century are only leap years if the year is dividable by 400. Year 2000 was a leap year.

The formula for calculating weekdays was created for the 1900s. To calculate weekdays after 31 December 1999 you have to add 6 to the answer.

Which day of the week did the Sydney to Hobart race start in 2004?

26 less 21 is 5 (date) + 6 (December) = 11. Less 7 = 4 + 4 (the year 04) = 8 = 1. Add 6 for the years of the 21st century. 1+6 = 7. The answer is 7 - Sunday.

For the 1700s: add four   For the 2100s: add four
For the 1800s: add two   For the 2200s: add two
For the 1900s: nothing   For the 2300s: nothing
For the 2000s: add six

Continue in the same pattern; six, four, two, zero.

The formula only works for dates after 14 September 1752. This is when the British Empire switched from the Julian to the Gregorian calendar.

Pi (π) and long strings of numbers

My deary Dolly, be no chilly
My love I beg you, be my nymph

Being able to remember hundreds of decimals of pi may be the most useless skill you can possess. And that is precisely why the phenomenon is so exciting. In 1845 Professor Fauvel-Gouraud created a system where he translated each number to a consonant. No need to learn the system – but here it is:

0 is s, 1 is t/d, 2 is n, 3 is m, 4 is r, 5 is l, 6 is j/ch, 7 is g/k, 8 is f/v/ph and 9 is p/b.

By translating the numbers into letters Fauvel-Gouraud created a poem of the first 155 decimals of pi. In between the consonants he put vowels and silent letters like "h". Listen to this:

My deary Dolly, be no chilly
My love I beg you, be my nymph
Rich honey charm(s and) move(s) a man
A cupola seen (off with a) fiery top
A cottage bamboo, a poem (or a) glee
A tassel vain (or) a sappy grape
A rare Albino mucky (and) fat
Jersey Geneva Genoa (or) Seva
A boy (or) peevish knave somehow rough
An unholy marine editing a siege
A copy faint (though) rough (and) savage
(An) Old woman a fine miss (or) a showy Jew
A heroic Sepoy may fire where he choose(s)
(An) able wholesale (and) heavy unanimity.
A hackney lame (or) lubbers feet
No very heavy sin.

The last two digits are incorrect, as they had not correctly calculated pi in 1845. Words in brackets have no numerical value. The first two lines of the poem - My DeaRy DoLy, Be No JiLi, My LoVe i BeG you, Be My NyMF.

This gives us nineteen consonants we can convert to numbers:
M DR DL B N JL M LV BG B M NMF =
3 14 15 9 2 65 3 58 97 9 3 238.

Today, it would have taken memory competitors three to four minutes to memorise 160 digits. Fauvel-Gouraud's method is still impressive though. The methods being used today are much stronger and effective. Most impressive, perhaps, is the sheer will power required to memorise something like the decimals of pi. The Indian Rajan Mahadevan set a new world record in 1985 by correctly recalling the first 31 811 decimals of pi. Psychologists in the US examined him to try to understand how he managed this feat. Rajan's reply: remembering numbers was like riding a bicycle. He knew how to do both, but could explain neither. The psychologists concluded Rajan was blessed, or cursed, with a special skill.

The recipe

150 years after Fauvel-Gouraud's charming poem, Hiroyuki Goto from Japan recalled 42 195 decimals of pi – the official world record until 2006. Here are the first hundred decimals of pi:

3. 14 15 92 65 35 89 79 32 38 46 26 43 38 32 79 50 28 84 19 71 69 39 93 75 10 58 20 97 49 44 59 23 07 81 64 06 28 62 08 99 86 28 03 48 25 34 21 17 06 79

Rajan's feat was phenomenal – but remembering the decimals of pi is not witchcraft. There are several recipes. In the 2005 World Memory Championships I sat behind Dr Yip Swe Chooi from Malaysia. In 1998 he recalled 60 000 decimals of pi. Unfortunately he made 44 mistakes and the record was never approved. Yip says it took him three months to memorise pi by using journeys and the Alternative Double System. In hindsight he actually regrets doing it and says he would rather memorise useful information. He has already memorised an entire English Dictionary and is planning to memorise the Bible.

To memorise long strings of numbers you can visualise associations from the ADS, with three associations (six digits) at each point in the journey. The first two digits becomes a person, the next two the action and the last two digits the person being subject to this action. To memorise the first twelve decimals of pi (141592 653589) we only need two points: The hallway and the stairway.

141592 are the first six digits. Hallway is the location. Bird is the person (14). Fishing is the action (15). Gutenberg is the second person (92). A bird is fishing Gutenberg in the hallway.

653589 are the following digits. Stariway is the location. John Cusack is the person (65). Escape is the action (35). Adam Gilchrist is the second person (89). Cusack escapes Adam Gilchrist in the stairway.

Ben Pridmore, the 2004 memory world champion had, in August 2005, set his sights on the world record in memorising pi. He had memorised almost 50 000 decimals when the news broke that a Japanese had perfectly recalled 83 431 decimals. The record is still not confirmed, but it is unlikely that Ben will try to break it. Ben Pridmore has, like other memory world champions, learnt methods to improve his memory. Ben uses the Triple System to memorise numbers. He visualises two associations at each point. This is what memorising the next 12 decimals (793 238 462 643) would look like using the Triple System:

Each number is converted to letters using the Triple System. The three first digits, 793, become l oo b. Add letters and get lubricate. And 238 = t i m. Add letters and we get timber. Visualise someone lubricating a timer. To remember which association comes first at each point we place the first one above or to the left of the second. At the next point, memorise 383 and 279. The number 462 = rat. 643 = cob. Visualise a rattlesnake gliding across the cobblestones.

Other memory methods

The story method

If you have you heard about memory methods before, you have probably heard of the story method, the link method or the initial-letter-word method. Up until now most memory books have described these methods. One reason that a lot of people see memory improvement books as a waste of time is that the methods seem difficult and tiring.

The story or link methods are, in my opinion, a lot less powerful than methods incorporating locations. I hardly ever use the story or link methods in competitions, but I have used them occasionally as a supplement to memorising for exams. Kim's game is a game you may have played. You look at ten objects for twenty to thirty seconds. The objects are then covered up and you are asked to recall what you saw. No need to memorise this example:

Scissors, toothbrush, pen, key, knife, eraser, pencil sharpener, glasses, ruler, paperclip.

The average person would normally remember four to seven items. To remember more than that we have to put the objects into a system: we use methods to help our natural memory. With the story method we, create a story based on the items:

The scissors chop the brush off the toothbrush. It gets hurt and a pen falls out of the handle. The pen gets up and draws a key. A knife flies by and embeds in the drawing. An eraser hangs from the knife handle. A massive pencil sharpener walks by and eats the ruler. Out the other end comes a paperclip.

The effectiveness of the story method can be questionable, as you don't have a system for where you store the knowledge. If you have lots of stories to remember for your exam you risk not finding them in your mind and you will forget most of them shortly after the exam. Previous memory books ignored this problem. I recommend that you always combine the method you use with a location when the knowledge is important - perhaps by visualising a keyword for each story in a logical place or a journey. Admittedly, the story method is cute, so try to create a story on the order of the planets, starting closest to the sun. Try to create an association for each planet before you create the story. Mercury, Venus, Earth, Mars, Jupiter, Saturn, Uranus, Neptune. Pluto is furthest away but has now been reclassified as a dwarf planet.

The link method

The link method ties words together, like a chain. It is similar to the story method, but is easily recognisable by the fact that each word is featured twice (apart from the first one). In the story method we only visualised information once. The link method ties each new word to the last. The link method can therefore be safer when we have to remember information in the correct order. To memorise the numbers 2190876355 using the link method, you could do it like this:

A swan (2) sits on a pole (1). The pole falls down on an axe (9). The axe splits a ball (0). The ball rolls into a snowman (8). The snowman jumps on a diving board (7). Under the diving board there is an elephant (6). The elephant is handcuffed (3) around its legs. Some handcuffs are hanging in a hook (5). The hook hangs off another hook (5).

Memory competitions are good indicators of how good the different methods are. Several competitors have used the link method in international memory competitions but have never done well; the location method is simply too strong. The best result achieved by using the link methods, as far as I am aware, in memorising the most decks of cards in an hour, is three. However, Ben Pridmore managed twenty-seven using journeys. The link method is not useless though, as it can work quite well for memorising speeches and alike. Our example above used the Single System with one image for each number – but there is no reason not to link several images together using the double or Triple System.

Acronyms and mnemonic devices

How much air in the tyres, how to beat the stock market, when to prune the rose bushes, how to make sure we drink enough water and much more. We have rules and acronyms for almost everything. An acronym is a word formed from the initial letter of other words, but pronounced like a normal word instead of being spelled out, as in NATO, ANZAC and Laser (Light Amplification by Stimulated Emission of Radiation).

In the chapter on memorising for exams you read about the acronym SPA as a way to remember the (order of the) three Greek philosophers Socrates, Plato and Aristotle. To remember the colours of the rainbow, starting from the outside, you get *Roy G Biv*: Red Orange Yellow Green Blue Indigo Violet. If you cannot quite remember Roy G Biv, you could instead think of *Richard Of York Goes Battling In Vain*. The more concrete the words, the easier it is to imagine the picture. Use the first thing that pops into your mind.

To make sure that the acronym stays in the long-term memory we can save the images in our existing long-term memory. Think of a logical place for the colours of the rainbow. Look for Roy G Biv or Richard Of York Goes Battling In Vain, *in the shower.* Now you will know where to look when you forget the colours of the rainbow.

Memory clues can be created without using the initial letters too. Twice a year you will be reminded a thousand times to adjust you clocks for daylight savings. Here is tip: in spring you move the time an hour forward. You also get all the garden furniture out. In autumn you turn the clock back an hour. The garden furniture goes back in the shed.

Poems

A well-known and useful method is the poem method - you create rhyme and rhythm from the information you wish to remember. Think of *Righty Tighty, Lefty Loosely* and you'll remember which way to turn the screwdriver. This poem could be useful for history students and quiz nights: *Columbus sailed the ocean blue, in fourteen hundred and ninety two.* Create a poem to avoid getting sick when visiting exotic places: *Cook it, fry it, peel it – or beat it.*

The thickest string on the guitar is E. Then we have A, D, G, B and finally E again. Try to create a rhyme or a verse from E, A, D, G, B and E.

The phonetic alphabet

The phonetic alphabet is Uniform-Sierra-Echo-Foxtrot-Uniform-Lima to know. When remembering letters you can use the phonetic alphabet as your associations for the letters. It can be used to memorise passwords, formulas and much more. Here is the official NATO version:

Alfa	Juliet	Sierra
Bravo	Kilo	Tango
Charlie	Lima	Uniform
Delta	Mike	Victor
Echo	November	Whiskey
Foxtrot	Oscar	X-ray
Golf	Papa	Yankee
Hotel	Quebec	Zulu
India	Romeo	

To learn the entire phonetic alphabet you can use a journey with twenty-six points. Place one association for each word at each point. Visualise an Alfa Romeo at the first point. It is important to create concrete images to make visualisation easier. Bravo is abstract. So imagine a group of football supporters cheering in the second point. At the third point you run into Charlie Chaplin. Next you see a body builder flexing his deltoid. This is how you can memorise the entire alphabet. It's done in a flash and later you will learn useful applications for the phonetic alphabet.

Networks

A location can be many different things. A network is a little used storage method that works well for memorising street names and geography. Here is an example on how to memorise the layout of a fictional town. To memorise the streets and buildings you can think of a large room – the lounge room will do. First of all, a cannon is firing at the far side of the room. The middle of the floor is flooded. The pond does not have a name, but it is wet nonetheless. At the far left of the lounge room is an old castle. Along the left wall a farmer is out harvesting. The Queen herself is out walking along the right wall. The wall behind you is entirely made of wood. Down to the right is a funny looking building, with a fox peeking out behind it.

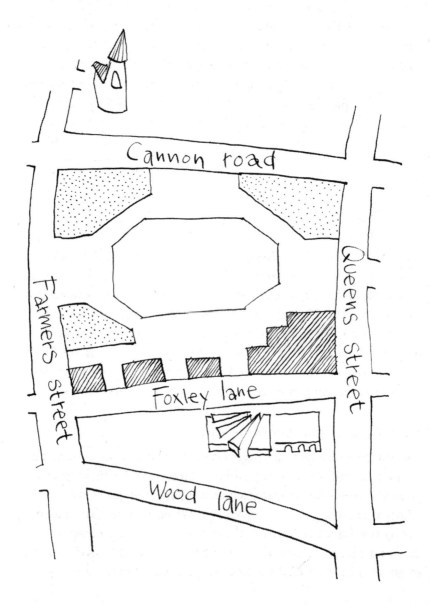

Mapping your keywords

You have probably been sitting an exam and seen pages of your textbook in your mind. You know exactly where on the page the answer is. Methods that have you map your keywords try to create a similar effect. The maps are like a sketch, with the key topic in the middle and keywords (or subtopics) spreading out like spider web. Let's say you are creating a map of keywords for physical education. The main topic, PE, should be sketched in the middle. Maybe add some colour or a symbol. Then draw some lines from the middle and add subtopics like warm-up, stamina, strength, and speed. Each category spreads out in a separate direction on the paper. Under each subtopic you then add keywords for each category. Under *speed* an obvious keyword would be *acceleration*. The next keyword (underneath acceleration) would be *max speed*. Under that again: *step & arm use*. Eventually you will end up with a map looking like an octopus. The core is physical education. Each subtopic has keywords for the most important concepts. In a sense you have created a location for the knowledge: the piece of paper. When you need to retrieve the information, you try to recall the map you drew. The map must be clear and precise for it to work optimally. Too cluttered and you will struggle to remember the keywords. If you have created a lot of maps of keywords it will be necessary to differentiate them to avoid confusion. Try to use illustrations and colours.

Does mapping your keywords work?

The purpose of mapping systems is to remember information. The purpose of journeys is to remember information. Using journeys you can, with some practice, remember two hundred or more words after having looked at them for fifteen minutes. Try remembering two hundred words in the correct order using a map – it could take hours or even days. In exams where I have used memory methods, I have recalled the knowledge from journeys. It is easy to pick and choose the necessary information - it is like looking through a book. I could stop and elaborate where necessary. Recalling maps with keywords all over them is much more difficult – probably more so for oral exams.

Some people are happy mapping keywords and concepts and I sometimes draw sketches or maps to get an overview of a project or something I am about to write. I never use systems like these to remember information. You can map your keywords as a supplement. Spreading your keywords out and drawing lines to connect them makes you think about the material. It helps you look at the big picture and choose keywords – much in the same way as Memo. One reason that maps or sketches may work better than traditional learning is simply that it creates a map - a form of location.

Alpha wave theory

People giving seminars on mapping methods quite often venture into questionable areas. They recommend listening to so-called alpha wave music to improve learning. Alpha wave music sounds like the ocean, but it's impractical to walk around listening to the sound of the ocean all day. Instead, we should focus on improving our learning in the mode the brain normally operates. If you are trying to memorise on the bus you need to be able to handle noise. You can't run home and turn on alpha wave music every time you want to learn. No amount of alpha wave music can get you to remember a quarter of a deck of cards. Maybe alpha wave music improves our learning marginally. Enough sleep is probably much more important. Alpha wave theory is a commercial gimmick like memory improvement pills from Israel.

Myths

Remembering vs understanding

Remembering is not enough, you have to understand it too. Some people are sceptical about my understanding of a subject when I speed-study. Criticisms of memory improvement methods are often based on misunderstandings and lack of knowledge on the topic. Normal rote learning may get you through the exam, but you will have forgotten most of it a few days later. Memo is different because you save the information in your long-term memory.

Takksemd til torbjørn for hjelp. Gode kjensler til laukeland dina skjørsæter norstrand evy svein-o storetor mamma og gjeraker for verdifull kritikk. Stor takk til bror hawk.

You can memorise the Norwegian paragraph above and recall it perfectly without having any idea about its content. That is, however, something totally different to understanding the first paragraph of this chapter. You can understand the subject if you know the language or the vocabulary. All subjects and professions have their own lingo. Maths has algebra, numbers and equations. Religions have their own words and meanings. Medicine can be incomprehensible to most people. To grasp the meaning of a subject is, most of all, about understanding the language. You will never fully comprehend something until you learn and understand the jargon. A saw is meant for sawing, memory methods are meant for remembering.

Memory methods are not required for you to understand something. If you cannot remember, it is hard to understand. You always have to remember things, regardless of the subject. You will not impress the teacher if you say Kuala Lumpur is the capital of China. So use memory methods to remember what you should remember. You will save a lot of time. Our limitations during exams are mostly related to what we can remember, not what we can understand.

You only use ten percent of your brain

Research by the psychologist Karl Lashley during the 1930s is one of the likely causes behind the perception that we only use ten percent of our brain. Lashley removed most of the cerebral cortex in the brain of rats and other animals and discovered that they could still learn specific skills. In another project neurologist placed electrodes straight on human brains and the results seemed to show large areas to be passive, leading them to conclude that humans only use ten percent of the brain. Some authors even claim that we only use one percent (Buzan, 2003).

Even if the rats could still learn specific skills after an operation like this, it is likely that other brain functions were destroyed. We only have to look at humans who have suffered some form of brain damage, to see that minor damage can result in severe handicap. Modern scanning equipment shows that Lashley and other scientists were wrong. Something as simple as reading out loud involves several parts of the brain. You use specific and different, parts of your brain during activities like eating, running or watching TV. At the end of the day you have used almost all parts of the brain.

One reason this myth has survived is that it has been repeated so often. It has turned into an undebatable fact. What is 100 percent of a brain's potential? How do we define the potential? It is impossible to say.

Did you know that you only use ten precent of your brain. Buy our book to improve your brain's potential, the ad says. Instead, we should rather listen to the brain expert who says that if your doctor wants to remove 90 percent of your brain, you should run like hell.

Photographic memory exists

I would define photographic memory as a permanent skill to quickly observe information and correctly recall information by recreating the picture in the mind. Like looking at a postcard for two seconds and then recalling all the details in the picture.

The most famous example of people with 'photographic memory' was the Russian journalist Shereshevskii (born in 1886), often called 'S'. The Russian neuro-pshycologist Aleksandr Luria studied his memory and wrote a book about him. S could study twenty numbers for forty seconds and recall them perfectly. He also managed to memorise fifty numbers in two to three minutes. One argument provided as proof of S's photographic memory was that he could recall strings of numbers for years after he had memorised them. The first thing that crossed my mind when I read about S, was how long it took him to memorise the information. When scientists claimed that S had photographic memory you would expect that he remembered the information after just a snapshot of observation. S memorised fifty numbers in two to three minutes. At the World Memory Championships in 2004 this would have placed him twenty-fourth out of twenty-four. S apparently used journeys, so do all memory competitors as far as I know.

To prove that anyone can easily improve his or her memory I did a project on Norwegian TV in 2006. The station found the random people: a hairdresser, an old bloke and the host of the show, a blonde girl. The hairdresser and the blond managed to remember 1005 decimals of pi (3.14 etc.) – after ten hours of memorising.

The retiree managed 120. He wasn't able to spend as much time on it as the girls, due to other commitments, but at least he remembered a lot more decimals than when he started. The competitors in international memory championships, the three people in the pi-project and myself have all learned how to improve our memory.

Most memory books are full of opinions based on myths around people like S. I feel that it is important to spend time rebutting the photographic memory myth, as it can stop you from believing that great memory is achievable for everyone.

The most provoking part about the myth is that several psychologist and doctors use S as an example as to why we should not desire good memory. They claim that S lived a sorry life and always waited for bigger and better things to happen. Maybe he was crazy, but good memory was not the cause nor did he have photographic memory.

Some people are indeed born with skills that make them remember lyrics or buildings perfectly. This skill, however, is confined to certain parts of the brain and the individuals often have trouble functioning properly in the society. This does not mean that improving your memory will cause you to go nuts. Where you born 'normal', you will never acquire problems simply because you remember more. In fact, the purpose of Memo is to spend less time and effort trying to remember.

Research shows that up to eight percent of pre-pubescent children have some sorts of photographic memory. One experiment is to show children illustrations from *Alice in Wonderland* and afterwards ask the children "how many stripes does the Cheshire cat have on its tail?" Some children would move their eyes to the part of the picture where they had spotted this detail and correctly answer the question. The children answered in present time, as if they were still looking at the picture. This phenomenon has not been found in older people, despite popular belief (Wetterberg, 2005).

Ten – eleven year olds occasionally take part in international memory competitions. Some have been able to remember a deck of cards in three to four minutes, which is impressive. The adults, however, who don't have photographic memory but rather rely on systems they have learned, can memorise a deck in forty seconds.

We have all experienced some form of 'photographic memory'. You may have been able to see entire pages of a textbook in your mind during an exam. This is not photographic memory according to my definition of the concept. Rather, it is an example of the brain's ability and inclination to create and remember layouts and systems. When you use journeys you are consciously taking advantage of this ability.

One person that has proved his exceptional memory skills for remembering *random* information is the Spaniard Ramón Campayo. In November 2004 he looked at forty binary numbers (0 and 1) for one second and recalled them all perfectly. The numbers where flashed on a computer screen in groups of three. This is probably the closest we will ever get to photographic memory. I do think more people could do it if they use a system and practice for years. The fact that he can do eighteen normal numbers (0 to 9) in one second arguably shows that Campayo uses a system. Visually there is very little difference between binary numbers and normal numbers.

Even if Ramón is really good in super-fast memory tasks, even I can beat him in memorising decks of cards. And as noted earlier: I don't have a photographic memory. In 2005 he failed twenty attempts in a row, trying to set a new world record for memorising binary numbers in two and three seconds. He is, after all, a human being, not a camera, but certainly an impressive performance!

The myth of photographic memory has been repeated so often that it is almost an indisputable fact – much the same way as the myth that we only use ten percent of our brain. Perhaps the media has yet to find a better explanation for good memory. One reason for the myth to be alive and well is the tricky situations many memory people come across. The general public is often surprised, and impressed, when shown a memory trick. If the method is then explained, some people feel cheated, as if expecting natural and magical skills. Suddenly the memory expert is no longer a person with good memory, but rather a cheat and a liar This is why many memory people choose not to explain their methods – to avoid upsetting people and let the public live with their belief in magic or 'photographic memory'.

We remember it all, we just need some help to retrieve it

Several psychologists believe that we can remember everything we have experienced. It is all in there; we just need some help to get it out. Many believe that hypnotists can help recover "forgotten" memories.

In a trial in 1990 George Franklin was convicted of the murder of Susan Nason, an eight-year-old girl who was killed in 1969. The key witness was Franklin's 28-year-old daughter Eileen. She supposedly recovered lost memories during therapy, relating to her father abusing and killing Susan. A judge later overturned the sentencing when it was discovered that Eileen had recalled the memories during hypnosis. Every detail she had recalled, had previously been published in newspapers; something that may have been the source of the confusion in her memory. Eileen had also discovered several other memories during the hypnosis – one being that her father had killed two other girls – which turned out to be false.

Participants in memory championships are not good at recalling memories – they are unusually good at memorising information.

They can therefore easily recall them, as the memories were saved in a system. The memorising is almost the entire job, recalling them is a piece of cake in comparison. There is no trance or hypnosis involved.

Listen to Mozart while eating goat cheese

Caffeine and nicotine have a short-term positive effect on the memory because they improve your concentration. Research also shows that small amounts of alcohol can, in some people, improve the memory. Most people would be able to remember five or six cards in a deck in the right order. Drinking three cups of coffee beforehand will only have marginal effect. If you learn Memo you will remember the entire deck. I am sure scientists could prove that eating saltbush would have a positive effect on your memory. I could probably find proof that plucking nose hair in small amounts can, in some instances, improve your memory. At least if the tweezers manufacturer sponsored the research.

It is amazing how many myths there are about what is good for our memory. Listen to Mozart while you eat goat cheese; angry people have better memory; use neon light in your reading lamp; and much more. Most of these would have no or at best a marginal effect on the memory. If you want a better memory you can just go on living the way you do and spend a little time learning some memory methods. Should you want to win memory competitions the most important part is to use a good system, practice and enough rest. A lot of seminars and memory books focus on all the aspects you have to consider when memorising. Seminar speakers and authors say you should focus on twelve factors: synesthesia, movement, association, sensuality, humour, imagination, numbers, symbolism, colours, order, positive images and exaggeration. When memorising you should use as many of these as possible.

That itself is an exaggeration. Memorising is much easier than that. You may become so restricted by all these things to consider that you never get started. The authors even have to use an acronym to remember which factors you should use to remember: *smashin' scope*. Some of the factors may work for you. Remember that time steals concentration.

Profiles and world records

Thousands of people around the world memorise decks of cards. Hundreds of them compete, or have competed, in international championships. England and German-speaking countries dominate the international competitions, but China, Australia and Norway are catching up and ready to overtake the reigning powers. So far, the biggest stars are from England:

Dominic O'Brien

Eight-time world champion Dominic revolutionised the sport with his Alternative Double System in the early 1990s. The Englishman made good money beating the Blackjack-tables in the US and Europe. He memorised 54 decks of cards (2808) in eleven hours and forty-two minutes in 2002 – making only 8 mistakes. These were not separate decks of cards, but rather 54 decks shuffled together.

Dominic has held all world records worth holding. For example: perfect recall of 280 random numbers after five minutes of memorising; 170 random words in 15 minutes and 128 spoken numbers. Dominic memorised all the questions and answers in two editions of Trivial Pursuit; he is yet to give a wrong answer to any of the 7400 questions.

Andi Bell

The distribution-centre worker from London is a triple world champion. In 2003 Andi memorised one hundred decks of cards in five hours. To make the recall quicker and more spectator friendly, Andi was asked about random cards from each deck of cards: which is card number thirty-two in the first deck, which is card number four in the second deck? He was correct 89 out of 100 times and he is planning to do a similar stunt soon. This time in four hours.

In 2004 Andi organised the 1st Memory World Cup to create a more fair sport – by removing biased events like those based on language. In 2004 he competed, with minimal training, in the World Memory Championships. Andi went for the world record in all events, but came up short in most of them. He did manage two world records though: 167 names and faces in 15 minutes and a deck of cards in 32.9 seconds. Both records have since been beaten, the latter by Andi himself. The record is now 31.16 seconds.

Simon Orton

Simon is one of the main supporters of functionalism in the memory society. Functionalists wish to use memory methods wherever they have practical applications – be it dancing or work. Simon will not shy away from competitions though, even if that means memorising useless information. In 2006 he defended his Australian Championships title.

Ben Pridmore

England has dominated the sport since 1990. Ben Pridmore has continued the tradition of Dominic O'Brien and Andi Bell. Because of a split in the society, two competing championships were held 2004: 1st Memory World Cup and World Memory Championships. Ben won them both. At the 1st MWC Ben set a new world record with thirteen decks of cards in thirty minutes. Along with the Southern-European competitors, Ben is the biggest opponent of functionalism. Ben supports what is often called absurdism – he prefers to memorise 'useless' information and nothing else.

World records

Jan Formann, from Denmark, held several world records in memorising numbers until the 2005 world championships. Now Englishmen and Germans dominate the official list of world records and records fell, like English cricketers, at the 2006 world championships. Generally, to break the records you must perfectly recall what you have memorised. In some events you get points deducted for every mistake you make. Andi Bell has memorised a deck of cards in 31.16 seconds and recalled it perfectly. Günther Karsten, from Germany, holds the record for ten minutes with 258 cards. In this event you only get 15 minutes to recall. In competitions I have managed 162 cards in ten minutes, placing me sixth on the world rankings. While training I have managed to do a deck of cards in 43 seconds. In an hour Ben Pridmore memorised 27 decks of cards for a total of 1404 cards.

Ben Pridmore also holds the record for the most random numbers in five minutes: 333. Several competitors claim to have managed 400 in training. To perform as well in competitions as during training is a rarity in memory sports. I have memorised over 110 random numbers in 60 seconds in training. The world record, which I set last year, for the most random numbers in 60 seconds is 72. Günther Karsten has the world record in memorising 1949 random numbers in one hour. In these two events you lose twenty points for every mistake you make. In the event *spoken numbers* you have to memorise as many numbers as possible, read out in one-second intervals - in the correct order. The 2005 World Champion Clemens Mayer (Germany), holds the record with 198 numbers. This is perhaps the most challenging event: the more numbers you try to remember, the bigger the risk of making a mistake and before you know it you end up with only ten to twenty points. Spoken numbers is also the event that demands the most from your ability to concentrate, as you don't set the pace yourself.

The most extreme record may be Ben Pridmore's record from 2005: 3705 binary numbers (0 and 1) in half an hour. Even more extreme is the fact that he beat his own record by 5 numbers in 2006. It means that you have to remember about two full pages of binary numbers, in the correct order. Being the absurdist that he is, this is obviously Ben's favourite event. Here are thirty binary numbers: 011010100001101011110110001010. And no, plain guessing won't do.

In several competitions, World Memory Championships being one, there are events that require memorising random words, names and faces, texts and fictional historical dates. These events can be hard to compare from one competition to another, as the words, names and texts are of varying degrees of difficulty. Several competitions have had a language bias, favouring certain competitors. Still, these events can be more useful to master than numbers and cards. Clemens Mayer has memorised the most names and faces. In fifteen minutes he memorised 181. The German Boris Konrad memorised 214 random words in the correct order, in fifteen minutes. My personal best is 207 during training. Astrid Plessl (Austria) managed 345 points in the event *text* in 2003. 345 points probably tells you nothing: in this event you memorise a text, line by line. Every full stop, comma, underline, capitalisation and italic must be memorised and recalled, in addition to the text obviously. Due to language differences this event has now been replaced by one memorising figures. Ben Pridmore also holds the record for memorising fictional historical dates. You have five minutes to memorise as many as you can. Afterwards you are given a list of the historical events, in random order and have to match the correct year to the correct event. One point for every correctly matched event and date –half a point deducted for every mistake. Ben managed an incredible 96 historical dates.

Memorising pi is not an official event in competitions - because pi is not a random number. People can memorise beforehand to gain an advantage. Memorising pi or the answers to quiz questions is not necessarily a test of who has got the best memory. To do this, the information must be random. No one can have the advantage of prior knowledge. Now you know the methods used in competitions. See you at the next international championships!

Appendix

For people who want or need to remember a lot of numbers we have created the following suggestions for associations to the entire Double System and Alternative Double System (ADS). Use some of the suggestions or create your own. If you only have to remember a few numbers for an exam or presentation, you don't need to learn all the associations – you learnt the basics earlier, so just pick the once you need from the list.

The Double System - only the first two consonants matter

Number			Association	Number			Association
00	F	F	FiFty Cent	13	N	B	NiB
01	F	N	FaN	14	N	R	NuRse
02	F	T	FooT	15	N	S	NoSe
03	F	B	FaBric	16	N	K	NooK
04	F	R	FeRry	17	N	L	NaiL
05	F	S	FiSh	18	N	M	NoMad
06	F	K	FaKe	19	N	G	NuGget
07	F	L	Flag	20	t	F	ToFfee
08	F	M	FoaM	21	t	N	TeNt
09	F	G	FiG	22	t	T	TaTtoo
10	N	F	iNFo	23	t	B	TaBlet
11	N	N	NaNny	24	t	R	Tree
12	N	T	NuT	25	t	S	TeaSpoon

Number			Association	Number			Association
26	t	K	TicKet	60	C	F	coffee
27	t	L	TuLip	61	C	N	CaNdy
28	t	M	ToM	62	C	T	CaT
29	t	G	TaG	63	C	B	CaB
30	B	F	BeeF	64	C	R	CoRkscrew
31	B	N	BeaN	65	C	S	CuShion
32	B	T	BaT	66	C	K	CockKatoo
33	B	B	BaBy	67	C	L	CoaL
34	B	R	BRick	68	C	M	CoMb
35	B	S	BuS	69	C	G	CoGnac
36	B	K	BucK	70	L	F	LiFejacket
37	B	L	BaLL	71	L	N	LaNce
38	B	M	BaMboo	72	L	T	LoTus
39	B	G	BaG	73	L	B	LaBrador
40	R	F	RaFt	74	L	R	LoRry
41	R	N	RaiNbow	75	L	S	LaSer
42	R	T	RaT	76	L	K	LocK
43	R	B	RaBbit	77	L	L	LiLy
44	R	R	ReaRend	78	L	M	LeMon
45	R	S	RoSe	79	L	G	LeG
46	R	K	RacK	80	M	F	MaFiaboss
47	R	L	RuLer	81	M	N	MooN
48	R	M	RoMan	82	M	T	MaT
49	R	G	RuG	83	M	B	MoBile
50	S	F	SaFe	84	M	R	MaRble
51	S	N	SaNdal	85	M	S	MaSk
52	S	T	STairs	86	M	K	MaKeup
53	S	B	SaBre	87	M	L	MuLe
54	S	R	SaRi	88	M	M	MuM
55	S	S	SeSame	89	M	G	MuG
56	S	K	SacK	90	g	F	GooFy teeth
57	S	L	SaLad	91	g	N	GuN
58	S	M	SaMurai	92	g	T	GoaT
59	S	G	SuGar	93	g	B	GoBlet

Number			Association	Number			Association
94	g	R	GuaRd	97	g	L	GeL
95	g	S	GooSe	98	g	M	GuM
96	g	K	GawK	99	g	G	GiGolo

The Alternative Double System (ADS)

Alternative Double System - remember that only the letters 'o i t e r s c l a g' have any value

			Person	Action
00	o	o	Ozzy Osborne	bookbinding
01	o	i	Poirot (Hercule)	oiling
02	o	t	Oliver Twist	photographing
03	o	e	Joey	obeying
04	o	r	Orangoutan	orbiting
05	O	s	Ostrich	oscillating
06	o	c	octopus	occupying
07	o	l	Osama bin Laden	bowling
08	o	a	Boa-snake	boarding the plane
09	o	g	Dog	jogging
10	i	o	Dido	Fido-walking (dog-walking)
11	i	i	pippi langstrømpe	bidding/dipping
12	i	t	Ian Thorpe	biting
13	i	e	miner	immersing/injecting
14	i	r	bird	ironing
15	i	s	fish	fishing
16	i	c	Ian Chapell	icing (a cake)
17	i	l	Ivan Lendl	building
18	i	a	Idi Amin	dialing
19	i	g	iguana	igniting
20	t	o	Tomboy	torturing
21	t	i	Tiger Woods	tieing
22	t	t	Tina Turner	putting
23	t	e	Thomas Edison	telephoning
24	t	r	Theodore Roosevelt	trapping
25	t	s	Tsar	tusseling
26	t	c	Tom Cruise	tucking
27	t	l	butler	nutlifting
28	t	a	Taxi driver	talking
29	t	g	tagger	tugging
30	e	o	demon	demonstrating

			Person	**Action**
31	e	i	neighbour	meditating
32	e	t	ET	betting
33	e	e	Bee	peeling
34	e	r	Errol Flynn	erasing
35	e	s	Eskimo	escaping
36	e	c	Edith Cowan	echoing
37	e	l	Elephant	melting
38	e	a	Earl	eating
39	e	g	Meg Ryan	begging
40	r	o	Robot	rowing
41	r	i	rhinoceros	riding
42	r	t	Ruth (Babe Ruth)	running
43	r	e	Reptile	reading
44	r	r	Robert Redford	brr (freezing)
45	r	s	Ringo Starr	brushing
46	r	c	Russel Crowe	rucksacking
47	r	l	Rod Laver	ruling
48	r	a	Rafael Nadal	Rafting
49	r	g	Rugby player	Rucking
50	s	o	Soldier	Soaping
51	s	i	Sikh	Sitting
52	s	t	Starfish	Stabing
53	s	e	Seal	sealing
54	s	r	Shrek	shrieking
55	s	s	Steven Spielberg	sustaining
56	s	c	Simon Crean	screwing/scratching
57	s	l	Slave	sleep
58	s	a	Saddam Hussein	sailing
59	s	g	Sugar Ray Leonard	suggesting
60	c	o	Cowboy	cooking
61	c	i	Cinderella	circling
62	c	t	Charlize Theron	cutting
63	c	e	Clint Eastwood	celebrating
64	c	r	Chris Rock	creeping
65	c	s	Cusack (John)	cushioning
66	c	c	Charlie Chaplin	ducking

			Person	**Action**
67	c	l	Cleopatra	clapping
68	c	a	Cat	carving
69	c	g	Cary Grant	cudgel hitting
70	l	o	Lord	loading
71	l	i	Lion	listening
72	l	t	Liv Tyler	fluttering
73	l	e	Leech	lending
74	l	r	Lionel Richie	lubricating
75	l	s	Bulls	blushing
76	l	c	Lucifer	lunching
77	l	l	Libby Lenton	lulling
78	l	a	Louis Armstrong	lassoing
79	l	g	Bulgarian	lugging
80	a	o	Mao	avoiding
81	a	i	Mailman	mailing
82	a	t	Ato Boldon	attacking
83	a	e	Albert Einstein	apeing
84	a	r	Andy Roddick	arresting
85	a	s	Arnold Schwartznegger	asking
86	a	c	Al Capone	packing
87	a	l	Ali	falling
88	a	a	Amazon	analysing
89	a	g	Adam Gilchrist	agonizing
90	g	o	God	gobble
91	g	i	Giraffe	guitar playing
92	g	t	Gutenberg	gutting
93	g	e	Gloria Estefan	gesturing
94	g	r	Giaan Rooney	grabbing
95	g	s	Gwen Stefani	gust blowing
96	g	c	Greg Chapell	hug collecting
97	g	l	George Lucas	gluing
98	g	a	Gillian Anderson	gaping
99	g	g	Germaine Greer	juggling

The Triple System

	As first digit	As second digit	As third digit	
1	N	a	N	a as in cat
2	T	e	T	e as in pet
3	B	i	B	i as in kitten
4	R	o	R	o as in tom
5	S	u	S	u as in puss
6	K	A	K	A as in hay
7	L	E	L	E as in bee
8	M	I	M	I as in high
9	gj	O	g	o as in low
0	f/th	oo	f/th	oo as in pool

If you are hooked

1 to 20 in Turkish

Can you count to twenty in Turkish? In five minutes you may be able to — if you use Memo.

Number		Pronoun-ciation	Associations	Some suggestions
1	Bir	Bir		Built-in-robe (b.i.r.)
2	Iki	Iki		
3	Üç	Utsch		Clutch
4	Dört	Dört		Dart
5	Beş	Besh		The Colour beige
6	Alti	Alte		
7	Yedi	Jedi		Jedi-knight
8	Sekiz	Sekis		Sack + ice
9	Dokuz	Dākus		Doc + US
10	On	Ān		Ant
11	On bir	Ān bir		11 to 19 you don't have to memorise, as it is just adding 'on' in front of 1 to 9.
12	On iki	Ān iki		-

Number		Pronoun-ciation	Associations	Some suggestions
13	On üç	Ān utsch	-	
14	On dört	Ān dört	-	
15	On beş	Ān besh	-	
16	On alti	Ān alte	-	
17	On yedi	Ān jedi	-	
18	On sekiz	Ān sekis	-	
19	On dokuz	Ān dākus	-	
20	Yirmi	Jirmi		Jimmy

Morse code

To make it easier to remember Morse code, I have developed a system where the dots and dashes are turned into words. Each dot is a vowel and each dash a consonant. It was a lot easier to make associations in Norwegian than in English (four more vowels), but by counting h as a vowel you'll find suggestions for most of the letters. Based on these letters we make words that we associate with the Morse code. The Morse code for A is • – (dot - dash). We create a two-letter words, vowel + consonant. For example AG (Attorney General). Should you forget what the Morse code for A is, you can think of the AG = vowel + consonant = dot + dash.

To make it logical, most words start with the same letter as the code for the letter it is representing. B = Beau (dash – dot – dot - dot), C = Cola (dash – dot – dash - dot).

Letter	Code	Word	Letter	Code	Word
A	• –	aG (Attorney General)	N	– •	No!
B	– • • •	Beau	O	– – –	TNT (dynamite)
C	– • – •	Cola	P	• – – •	aBBa
D	– • •	Doe	Q	– – • –	crab
E	•	E	R	• – •	oRe
F	• • – •	hiFi	S	• • •	hoe
G	– – •	Gnu	T	–	T (short of Time, think about a watch)
H	• • • •	four (four dots - sailboat)	U	• • –	oUt
I	• •	ai!	V	• • • –	hood
J	• – – –	odds	W	• – –	oWl
K	– • –	Cow	X	– • • –	sail
L	• – • •	aLoe	Y	– • – –	Yolk
M	– –	MP (Member of Parliament)	Z	– – • •	sloe

The advantage of the method is that the number of letters corresponds with the number of dots and dashes in the Morse code. You simply just turn the word back in to dots and dashes. When you have used the Morse code for a while, the knowledge becomes automatic and you will not longer have to look through the visualisations every time. The problem with introducing this in the military is to work out what the recruits are going to do for the next week.

Binary numbers

Computers do all their calculations using binary numbers. Only the numbers 0 and 1 exist in a binary system. We rarely come across the system on a daily basis, but being able to memorise binary numbers actually has some practical applications. I used the system when a friend flipped a coin one hundred times and asked me to recall the order of heads and tails. Heads was memorised as 0, tails as 1. Seriously, binary numbers are generally useless for your memory, even though it is an event at competitions. It could still be useful to know though and you may find more useful applications for it.

We can divide binary numbers into groups of three digits and transform them like this:

000 = 0	100 = 4
001 = 1	101 = 5
010 = 2	110 = 6
011 = 3	111 = 7

You have already learned the Alternative Double System. Add two groups of three binary numbers to get a double number. 000 110 becomes 0 6. Using the ADS we get octopus (0=o, 6 = c). Longer binary numbers can be memorised by using person + action. 110 011 011 111 becomes 6 3 3 7. Visualise like this: Clint Eastwood (63) melting (37). Here are some associations:

Binary	Number	Person	Action
011 010	32	ET	betting
011 011	33	Bee	peeling
011 100	34	Errol Flynn	erase
011 101	35	Eskimo	escape

Binary	Number	Person	Action
011 110	36	Edith Cowan	echo
011 111	37	Elephant	melting
100 000	40	Robot	rowing
100 001	41	Rhinoceros	ride

The rest you can work out based on the Alternative Double System.

Practical use

Braille can easily be memorised using the binary system. Braille has six points where there either is a dot or nothing. Make the dot 1 and no dot 0. Using the binary system the Braille letter S becomes 011 100 = 34 = ER. You can use the phonetic alphabet as associations for the letters. The letter E in Braille becomes 100 010 in binary, which is 42 in the ADS = RT. Imagine Ruth walking in Ecco-shoes (Echo is E in the phonetic alphabet). Save the Braille in a journey until it becomes automatic.

The binary system can be used to memorise computer programming. You can even use binary to learn how to play the flute.

Wonders of the World

To memorise the seven wonders of the ancient world, you can create a seven-point journey. Make one or two simple associations for each wonder. For example a balloon (Babylon) on a wall (walls). Once you have created the associations, you memorise them in the journey.

- Babylon's Walls and Hanging Gardens
- Temple of Artemis at Ephesus
- Statue of Zeus at Olympia
- The Great Pyramid Of Giza (Egypt)
- Mausoleum of Masussollos at Halicarnassus
- Colossus of Rhodes (Statue of the Sun God Helios)
- Lighthouse of Alexandria

This is the oldest list of the seven most famous wonders of the classical-oriental world. The number seven is thought to have magical powers. Later, other wonders were added, like Noah's Ark, Coliseum in Rome and Hagia Sophia in Constantinople (Istanbul).

Countries and capitals in South America

What is the capital of Suriname? Try memorising the capital and location of all the countries in South America. Use the same recipe as in the Geography chapter.

Country - Capital	Associations	Suggestions – Country	Suggestions – Capital
Chile – Santiago		Chilli	Santa Claus
Argentina – Buenos Aires		Maradona	Airbag
Uruguay – Montevideo		Urn	Video
Brazil – Brasilia		Coffee	Coffee
French Guyana – Cayenne		French flag	Kayak
Suriname – Paramaribo		Sour cream	Parachute
Guyana – Georgetown		Guy	George (+city)
Venezuela – Caracas		Venison	Car
Colombia – Bogotá		Coca Cola	Bog
Ecuador – Quito		Globe	Key
Peru – Lima		Pear	Lime
Bolivia – La Paz		Bolt	Lap
Paraguay - Asunción		Para glider	Asteroid

Bibliography

Bell, Andi. 2000. *Memory book*. London: Carlton books

Buzan, Tony. 2003. *Head First: 10 Ways to Tap into Your Natural Genius*. London: Thorsons Publishers

Karlsen, Pål Johan. 2004. *Slik får du bedre hukommelse*. Oslo: Aschehoug

Luria, Alexander. 1987. *The mind of a mnemonist*. Harvard University Press

O'Brien, Dominic. 1993. *How to Develop a Perfect Memory*. London: Pavilion Books

O'Brien, Dominic. 2001. *Lær å huske*. Oslo: Gyldendal

Passer, Michael & Ronald Smith. 2004. *Psychology – The Science of Mind and Behavior*. New York: McGraw-Hill

Tarantino, Quentin. 1994. *Pulp Fiction*. London: Faber&Faber

Wetterberg, Peter. 2005. *Hukommelsesboken*. Oslo: Gyldendal

For more information about Memo – don't forget www.oby.no/au (it is in English)

Acknowledgements

Thanks to Susie, Håkon, Simon, Lucy, Jeremy, Greer, Mark, Torfinn, Siri and Lars Eirik for helping to make the Australian edition as good as possible.